NURTURING INTELLIGENCES CORE LITERATURE SERIES

Teaching Guide for Paul Fleischman's

Joyful Noise:
Poems for Two Voices

Brian A. Haggerty

Innovative Learning Publications

Addison-Wesley Publishing Company

Menlo Park, California ■ Reading, Massachusetts ■ New York
Don Mills, Ontario ■ Wokingham, England ■ Amsterdam ■ Bonn
Paris ■ Milan ■ Madrid ■ Sydney ■ Singapore ■ Tokyo
Seoul ■ Taipei ■ Mexico City ■ San Juan

Senior Editor: Lois Fowkes
Project Editor: Jean Nattkemper
Production Director: Janet Yearian
Production Coordinator: Claire Flaherty
Design Manager: Jeff Kelly
Text and Cover Design: Paula Shuhert
Production and Illustration: Graham Metcalfe

Acknowledgments

Thanks are due to numerous colleagues and friends at San Diego City Schools who, over the years, have made suggestions and offered encouragement regarding the development of multiple intelligences-based teaching materials. They will find many of their suggestions reflected in this literature teaching guide. Particular thanks are offered to Bob Grossman, for suggestions regarding how to teach middle school students about the world of insects; to Fran Slowiczek, for providing information about surface tension and compass needles; to Beverly Trust and Ray Conser for information about biological supply houses and literature about insects; and to Momiji Seligman, for suggestions about musical selections and information about rhythmic bodily movements.

This book is published by Innovative Learning,™ an imprint of the Alternative Publishing Group of Addison-Wesley Publishing Company.

ISBN 0-201-49058-7

1 2 3 4 5 6 7 8 9 10-ML-98 97 96 95 94

Contents

Introduction

The literature titles selected for the *Nurturing Intelligences* Core Literature series represent excellence in reading for students in grades 4–12. The titles have been chosen because they meet a variety of specific criteria, either individually or collectively.

- Each selection has been recognized through one or more professionally acknowledged processes as having especially commendable quality. A large number of the titles selected, for example, are Newbery Medal Winners, Newbery Honor Books, or American Library Association Notable Books. In addition, the selections are included on many state department of education and local school district recommended reading lists.

- Each selection lends itself to cross-curricular teaching. It permits teachers to draw on and help students develop understanding in a variety of traditional school subject areas.

- Many individual selections represent the literary contributions of specific ethnic or cultural groups or offer opportunities for understanding particular cultures. Taken together, the selections reflect the cultural diversity of our nation and world and the richness of the cultural heritage in which we share.

- The selections represent a variety of literary types and genres, including historical and contemporary realistic fiction, modern fantasy and science fiction, folklore and myth, biography and poetry.

The teaching activities and suggestions included in each Literature Teaching Guide have been informed in good measure by insights drawn from the theory of multiple intelligences. MI theory, which has been developed by cognitive psychologist Dr. Howard Gardner and his colleagues at Harvard University, proposes that every normal individual comes to knowledge in different ways and that each person blends these ways of knowing in a unique fashion. It proposes further that successful teaching appeals to the different intelligences and combinations of intelligences that each student possesses.

Dr. Gardner has described this rich understanding of human intellectual potential in *Frames of Mind* (3d ed. Basic Books, 1993). A summary of MI theory and its implications for classroom teaching may be found in the book that serves to introduce the *Nurturing Intelligences* Core Literature Series: *Nurturing Intelligences: A Guide to Multiple Intelligences Theory and Teaching* (Addison-Wesley, 1995). This teaching guide includes a concise overview of MI theory. It also proposes specific teaching and learning activities which are suggested by the literature selection and through which teachers may help students develop their multiple intelligences.

This literature teaching guide for Paul Fleischman's Newbery Award-winning poetry collection *Joyful Noise: Poems for Two Voices* is intended for use by teachers of middle-school students, that is, students in grades 6–8.

Introducing *Joyful Noise: Poems for Two Voices*

"For me the initial delight in poetry is in the surprise of remembering something I had forgotten," wrote Robert Frost, "or remembering something I didn't know I knew."

In *Joyful Noise: Poems for Two Voices,* Paul Fleischman evokes the taken-for-granted world of insects and, in the process, helps us rediscover a sense of wonder many of us surely possessed before we became consumed with the mundane concerns of daily human existence.

In 14 poems, intended to be read aloud by two voices, Fleischman puts remarkable facility with language and fertile imagination at the service of careful entomological research to paint in words vivid and accurate pictures of his insect subjects. With him we delight in the exuberance of grasshoppers stepping out into spring. We marvel at the confidence of water striders moving effortlessly across the surface of the water. We sympathize with mayflies trying to crowd an adult lifetime into a single day. We admire the artistry of fireflies dabbing the dark night canvas with flashes of light. We envy the comfortable complacency of the house cricket, blithely ignoring the changes of seasons and their attendant perils.

The 14 poems call forth a full range of emotions, from enthusiasm to melancholy, from boisterous joyfulness to profound sadness. Each poem stands on its own, unique in tone, style, and theme. Taken together, they lyrically celebrate a world we did not know we knew.

About Paul Fleischman

Paul Fleischman came early to appreciate the musical quality of words and ways in which words can be combined to please the listening ear as well as the discerning eye.

His father, award-winning children's book writer Sid Fleischman, read his stories aloud to his son and his daughters chapter-by-chapter, as he wrote them. Shortwave radio broadcasts from faraway countries brought him the exotic sounds of words he did not understand but in whose music he delighted.

A hand printing press taught him the beauty of the shapes of words and of their look on a page. Sculptures he fashioned out of found materials strengthened his appreciation of form and helped him develop principles of design.

Mr. Fleischman's early experiences have served him well. His 16 books—historical and contemporary fiction, fantasy, natural history, and poetry—demonstrate his remarkable sensitivity to the power of words not only to inform the mind and stimulate the imagination, but to please the ear and satisfy the eye.

Many of his books, including *The Half-a-Moon Inn, The Borning Room, Graven Images, Path of the Pale Horse,* and *Saturnalia,* have received awards reserved for the best in children's literature. None has been more widely recognized than his *Joyful Noise: Poems for Two Voices,* the 1989 Newbery Medal winner, a 1988 American Library Association Children's Notable Book, and a 1988 *Boston Globe-Horn Book* Fiction/Poetry Award Honor Book.

While living for a time in New Hampshire, Fleischman took pleasure in playing music with a small group of musicians. He found that playing was more fun than merely listening to music and that playing with others was more exciting than playing alone. Similarly, Paul Fleischman's poetry is meant to be read aloud rather than silently, to be read with others rather than alone.

Note: All page references to *Joyful Noise: Poems for Two Voices* in the teaching guide correspond to the Harper Trophy Book paperback edition (Harper & Row, 1992). A cassette tape, *Joyful Noise and I Am Phoenix: Poems for Two Voices,* by Paul Fleischman, performed by John Bedford Lloyd and Anne Twomey, 1990, is available from Harper & Row (10 East 53rd Street, New York, NY 10022).

Teaching Suggestions

The teaching suggestions offered in this core literature teaching guide seek to help students develop the rich variety of intellectual competences they possess. The guide draws much of its inspiration from the theory of multiple intelligences, first proposed by Howard Gardner in 1983 and subsequently refined by Gardner and his colleagues, who have applied its insights to a variety of teaching situations.

Multiple Intelligences Theory

Multiple intelligences theory holds that intelligence is pluralistic, not unitary, in design—that is, that intelligence is many and not one. This understanding differs notably from the position long taken by many psychologists, who have considered intelligence to be a single general ability, found in varying degrees in all normal individuals and applicable in any problem-solving situation.

According to Gardner and his colleagues, the traditional understanding of intelligence fails to account for the many forms that intellectual accomplishment takes in cultures around the world and for the variety of symbol systems through which that accomplishment is achieved and expressed. Gardner proposes that intelligence may be most accurately understood as **the ability to solve problems or to fashion products that are valued in one or more cultures.**

To determine which human competences might qualify as intelligences, Gardner and his colleagues consulted evidence from a wide variety of independent research traditions, including those of cognitive developmental psychology, neurology, biology, anthropology, psychometrics, and experimental psychology. By correlating the results of their research, they have developed a number of signs by which to judge whether a particular competence might qualify as an intelligence. Among those signs are

- the potential isolation of the competence by brain damage.

- the existence of special populations—prodigies, idiots savants—in whom the competence is manifested to an extraordinary degree or in whom it is uniquely spared.

- the identification of the competence with one or more core operations, that is, information-processing mechanisms peculiar to specific kinds of input.

- the ability to trace a distinctive developmental history for the competence through which all normal as well as gifted individuals pass.

- the susceptibility of the competence to be represented in a symbol system, such as the linguistic, numerical, gestural, and pictorial systems we humans have developed to capture and communicate meaning.

To date Gardner and his co-workers have proposed that at least seven human competences, or skills universal to the human species, exhibit all or most of these signs. (See Figure 1.1.) The content of the seven intelligences as well as some typical "end-states" resulting from their skillful use may be summarized as follows:

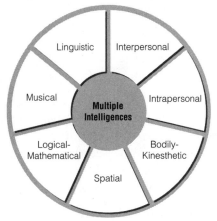

Figure 1.1 The Seven Intelligences of Multiple Intelligences Theory

Linguistic intelligence includes sensitivity to the meaning of words; sensitivity to the order among them; sensitivity to their sounds, rhythms, inflections, and meter; and sensitivity to the functions of language. Linguistic intelligence is manifested by skillful writers—novelists, poets, essayists, historians, literary critics, and the like—and by effective orators as well as by persons who have developed a refined appreciation of written and spoken expression.

Musical intelligence entails sensitivity to pitch (melody); sensitivity to rhythm; and sensitivity to timbre, or the characteristic qualities of a tone. This intelligence is required of successful composers, instrumentalists, singers, and conductors as well as of discerning listeners.

Logical-mathematical intelligence includes the ability to discern logical or numerical patterns as well as the ability to prosecute extended lines of reasoning. Logical-mathematical intelligence is demonstrated by mathematicians; by scientists, for whom analysis is the path to understanding; by computer programmers; and by individuals involved in a variety of business-related enterprises such as accounting, analysis of fiscal reports, market analysis, financial forecasting, and inventory management.

Spatial intelligence encompasses a variety of abilities, including the capacity to manipulate or mentally rotate forms or objects perceived; the capacity to perceive forms or objects accurately and recognize instances of the same element; the capacity to conjure up mental imagery and then to transform that imagery; the capacity to produce a graphic likeness of forms or objects perceived; and sensitivity to the tension, balance, and composition that characterize visual and spatial displays in the graphic arts and in many natural elements. Spatial intelligence is required of physicists, engineers, architects, fine and commercial artists, inventors of tools, mechanics, and chess players.

Bodily-kinesthetic intelligence includes the ability to handle objects skillfully and the ability to use one's body in differentiated and skilled ways for functional or expressive purposes. Skilled dancers, athletes, and actors demonstrate this intelligence, as do surgeons, pianists, and violinists, and a variety of craftspersons.

Intrapersonal intelligence is characterized by the ability to build a reliable working model of oneself, including one's strengths and weaknesses, and to make decisions based on that model. Intrapersonal intelligence is required to make appropriate decisions in life, such as career choices.

Interpersonal intelligence is characterized by the ability to distinguish among the moods, temperaments, motivations, and intentions of others and to act upon that knowledge. Interpersonal intelligence is required of anyone who is confronted with the task of trying to influence the behavior of others along desired lines, thus of political and religious leaders, work force managers and supervisors, counselors and therapists, teachers and parents.

Howard Gardner proposes that in attempting to solve problems and create products, every normal individual has a repertoire of skills that includes at least the seven relatively independent intellectual capacities just described and that each capacity is characterized by its own distinctive modes of thinking. Although he maintains that each of the intelligences he has identified is relatively autonomous, or independent of the others, he also affirms that intelligences typically work in harmony. Any sophisticated adult role, he points out, requires a blending of several of the intelligences. A skilled actor, for example, needs not only the bodily-kinesthetic intelligence to assume another persona but also the interpersonal intelligence required to communicate with audiences, the intrapersonal intelligence needed to select appropriate roles, and the linguistic intelligence required to deliver lines effectively. A skilled physicist needs not only the spatial intelligence required to visualize the make-up of the physical world but also the logical-mathematical intelligence to analyze evidence and develop hypotheses and the linguistic intelligence to communicate findings, either orally or in writing.

Each intelligence specified in multiple intelligences theory includes a number of core operations. The exercise of a particular intelligence, however, does not require the demonstration of each of those operations. Some individuals skilled in an intellectual domain may be stronger in a particular operation than in others. A skillful orator, for example, may not be especially adept at writing. A skilled engineer may well lack the ability required to be a skilled sculptor.

Finally, although Gardner finds that each intelligence he has identified is demonstrated in a wide variety of cultures, he also holds that intelligences may manifest themselves differently in different cultures. Linguistic intelligence, for example, may manifest itself in writing in one culture, in storytelling in another, and in the possession of a powerful verbal memory in a third.

How—indeed whether—a particular intelligence will surface in individuals depends on at least two factors: whether the individual is endowed with the biological predisposition to find or solve problems in a given domain *and* whether the individual's culture elicits that predisposition or nurtures that domain. Would Michael Jordan have become a premier basketball player had he been born, say, in the Bahamas rather than in the United States? Would Gary Kasparov have become the world's best chess player had he been born in Bolivia rather than in the then-Soviet Republic of Azerbaijan? Intelligence, then, is a matter not only of potentials inside the head but also of opportunities for learning outside, in the culture.

This literature teaching guide, along with the other guides that make up the *Nurturing Intelligences* Core Literature Series, is intended to provide students with a rich variety of learning opportunities. By offering a wide range of teaching and learning activities, it seeks to build upon the students' intellectual endowments—their predispositions in particular domains—to help them cultivate the full range of human intellectual competences. If individuals succeed in the world to the degree that they develop and exploit their potentials, the type of educational approach offered in this guide and in the entire core literature series has an important contribution to make.

Teaching Guide Organization

For each of the 14 poems of *Joyful Noise: Poems for Two Voices* and for an introductory section on poetry writing, this literature teaching guide offers suggestions for teaching and learning activities suitable at three stages of study: before, during, and after the reading. At each stage the activities are intended to draw from a variety of traditional subject areas, thus encouraging cross-curricular teaching, and to capitalize on the wide variety of intelligences that students have the potential to develop.

Before the Reading

Activities at this stage are intended to arouse the students' curiosity about the poem and to activate their prior knowledge or provide background information they may need to understand or appreciate the poem. The prior knowledge you may need to activate and the background information you may need to provide deal not only with matters of fact *(How do grasshoppers make their distinctive sounds? Why do fireflies make small, flashing lights?)* but also with matters of perspective or point of view *(How might it feel to walk upon water? Why might the queen bee and the worker bee see things differently?)*, with expectations regarding literary form, and with essential vocabulary.

Some observers report that reading teachers often slight or skip the preparation phase of reading instruction, maintaining they do not have enough time for it. In fact, research indicates that preparation for reading

that focuses on concepts central to understanding the selection to be read, but which students do not possess or might not recall without cues, leads to greater reading comprehension.

During the Reading

Activities at this stage are intended to help students comprehend what is read to them or what they are reading themselves. These activities include various reading strategies described, as well as questions you might ask your students to encourage them to talk about the poem and to help them build their proficiency in reading. During the Reading activities also include suggestions for helping students increase their vocabulary comprehension.

After the Reading

Activities at this stage are intended to help the students deepen their appreciation of the poems and make them their own. Although the activities suggested often involve language arts—listening, speaking, reading, writing—they encourage the natural connections that exist between language arts and such traditional school subject areas or disciplines as mathematics, science, social studies, physical education, and the visual and performing arts.

There is no need to lead the students through the After the Reading activities in the order in which they are described. The activities may be conducted in any order you deem useful or appealing to your students.

The students' class schedules may help determine when it is most appropriate to use specific teaching activities. In some classroom situations, relatively large blocks of time may be devoted to language arts classes or to combined language arts and social studies classes. In such cases, teachers and students will be able to participate in a substantial number of the activities described during the blocks of time available.

In other situations, the students' class day may be divided into shorter time periods, each assigned to a specific subject area. In those cases, some of the activities may be used during language arts class and others during social studies, visual or performing arts, music, physical education, mathematics, and science classes. The Teaching Guide Overview that follows indicates not only the intelligences that the activities may help students develop but also the traditional school subject areas from which each suggested teaching activity is drawn. If this latter approach is followed, you may find that Paul Fleischman's *Joyful Noise* and this teaching guide help provide thematic unity for your students' learning experiences.

It is not necessary that all the students take part in all the activities. The literature teaching guide, for example, often provides more than one activity designed to help students develop a particular intelligence or blend of intelligences. In that case, choose, or allow students to choose, from among the activities available or devise other activities of your own, using those provided as models.

Nor is it necessary, in many instances, that the entire class group participate in each activity together. Consider establishing learning centers—stations or corners of the classroom equipped with appropriate materials and resources and devoted to specific activities or types of activities—and permitting small groups of students, or individual students, to participate in the activities they choose in the order they choose.

You might establish a different set of learning centers for each of the poems of *Joyful Noise*. Or you might establish learning centers that correspond to the linguistic, musical, logical-mathematical, spatial, and bodily-kinesthetic intelligences and arrange for the appropriate activities for each section to be conducted at those centers. Let the students help you decide how to set up the learning centers. If you establish learning centers, make sure you give the students clear, concise directions regarding the activities to be carried out at each center so they are able to work with a minimum of direction from you.

Finally, although the teaching guide follows the order in which the poems are printed in *Joyful Noise*, so long as the introductory poetry activities (see Introduction) are taught first, the poems may be taught in any order you deem appropriate. Note, however, that directions for some activities that are repeated may be spelled out more completely for the poems described early in the teaching guide than for the poems described later.

Reading Strategies

It may be effective to introduce each poem of *Joyful Noise* to your students by enlisting the help of a colleague or friend to read the poem with you, recording your reading of the poem in advance on an audiotape and playing it for the students. Or you might enlist the cooperation of one of your students who is a skilled reader and prepare an oral presentation of the poem in two voices.

Set the stage for your tape playback or reading by helping students apply their imaginations to the poem. Ask them, for example, to imagine what it might feel like to be able to hop, jump, and vault at will, the way grasshoppers seemingly do. Or ask which books they might choose to eat, the way book lice do.

After introducing the poem, allow each student time to read the poem silently. Then pair the students and encourage the pairs to prepare to read the poem aloud, for small groups and for the whole class.

To assist the students, have pairs listen to a tape-recorded version of the poem you have prepared with the help of a colleague or friend as they follow the text in their copies of *Joyful Noise*. (A cassette tape, *Joyful Noise and I Am Phoenix*, by Paul Fleischman, performed by John Bedford Lloyd and Anne Twomey, is available from Harper & Row.) Then record the student pairs as they read selections aloud and play their recordings back to them. Encourage the pairs to practice their performances until they can demonstrate an acceptable level of fluency.

If students initially have difficulty reading entire poems in two voices for their classmates, divide poems into sections of appropriate length and have pairs present the sections assigned to them. Students who may initially be shy about presenting poems orally might be allowed to play back to the class their recordings of Fleischman's poems until they have built up their confidence sufficiently to read before their classmates.

If some students have greater difficulty than others in presenting poems orally to their classmates, pair those who have difficulty reading orally with those who are comparatively skilled in this process.

Whatever approaches to reading the poems you take, encourage your students to create personal dictionaries. Have them copy into notebooks words and phrases with meanings they do not understand or pronunciations unclear to them. Have them leave room to insert definitions and pronunciation keys. At appropriate intervals, have the students share—with the class, with reading group members, or with reading partners—the words and phrases they have copied. Encourage them to seek from each other suggestions about meanings and pronunciation. Emphasize the advantages of using context clues to determine word meaning.

If you think it appropriate for your students' reading abilities, you might also distribute copies of the Glossary found at the end of this core literature teaching guide. In that case, explain that, unlike a dictionary, a glossary indicates the meaning of words in a particular story or piece of writing, not all the possible meanings.

Cooperative Learning

Intelligence, Howard Gardner has concluded, cannot be properly conceptualized apart from the context in which individuals live. Intelligent activity, then, is the result of interaction between individual biological potentials and cultural opportunities.

Likewise, Gardner suggests, intelligence cannot be fully understood apart from the human and inanimate objects the individual uses to solve problems or fashion products. Intelligent activity is rarely the result of humans working alone, inside their heads. Rather, it most often results from interaction with other individuals and with all kinds of inanimate objects and prosthetics.

Gardner and others engaged in examining the nature of intelligence refer to this phenomenon as "distributed intelligence." Intelligence, they suggest, is not restricted to the contents of the individual's mind but is distributed in other persons upon whom the individual can call for thinking out problems; making decisions; and recalling facts, concepts, and procedures. It also is distributed in the tools used by productive individuals, from notebooks and pencils to mainframe computers, from wheelbarrows to transit cranes.

One of the most effective ways of recognizing and capitalizing on the distributed nature of intelligence in teaching is *cooperative learning,* the instructional use of small groups of students who work together to solve problems and create products. This teaching guide suggests numerous specific ways in which you may use the approaches and techniques of cooperative learning to help your students read the poems of *Joyful Noise* with understanding and develop their multiple intelligences.

Simply having students work in groups rather than individually to complete specific tasks, however, does not assure that students will cooperate nor does it assure that they will take advantage of the distributed nature of intelligence. Here are several suggestions to help you use cooperative learning to the advantage of your students:

- Establish groups that range in size from two to six. Larger groups might offer a greater mix of abilities and expertise from which students may draw, but require more refined social skills on the part of students than do smaller groups. The availability of materials may dictate the size of groups, as may the time available to solve a problem or fashion a product. When only a short period of time is available, establish smaller cooperative groups, which can get organized and operate more quickly than larger groups.

- Group students heterogeneously. Include in each group students with high, medium, and low levels of ability in the specific domains in which students are asked to solve problems or create products. Include as well students with different working styles, that is, students who are confident as well as those who are tentative, students who are persistent as well as those who tend to become easily frustrated, and so on.

- Give students the opportunity to work cooperatively with every other student in the classroom. It is not necessary to change the composition of cooperative groups each time students are presented with a new instructional task, but, during the course of a school semester or year, every student should work with every other student.

- Arrange individual cooperative groups in the classroom in such a way that group members can easily share materials and can see and hear each other comfortably, without distracting, or being distracted by, other groups.

- Specify clearly the problem to be solved or the product to be created. Define concepts, explain procedures, and give examples to make sure students understand what is expected of them.

- Specify the collaborative skills students may need to complete the assigned or suggested task. Although the specific responsibilities or roles to be fulfilled may vary according to the problems posed or products expected, make sure students know that when they report their results to their classmates, they will have to indicate how each group member contributed to the result.

- Set standards of behavior for cooperative groups. Tell students to

  remain with their groups

  speak to one another by name

  talk in a way that does not disturb other groups

  give everyone in the group a turn to speak

  listen carefully to what everyone in the group has to say

  evaluate other group members' ideas rather than criticize other group members

  encourage everyone in the group to contribute

  check to make sure every group member understands the group's solutions to problems

- Observe groups carefully to determine problems they may have in completing the task or in working collaboratively. Clarify directions and procedures as needed. Intervene only when it appears that a group will not be able to work its way through its problems.

- Give students opportunities to summarize what they learned as well as to evaluate how effectively they collaborated.

Teaching Activities

Most of the teaching activities suggested in this teaching guide will be familiar to classroom teachers, if not in precise content, at least in general form. The following are some suggestions for conducting specific activities:

Guided Group Discussion

Middle school students often are responsive to discussion in large and small groups. Here are some hints for leading guided discussions:

- Ask questions of the entire group—the whole class or the smaller reading group. After asking each question, pause for a moment and then call on an individual for an answer. If you call on a student first and then ask your question, you run the risk of losing the attention of the rest of the group.

- Do not allow all the students to answer at once. Instead insist that the students wait to be called on.

- Give every student the opportunity to participate in discussions.

- Do not confuse the speed with which some students may be able to respond to questions with the substance of learning. Allow sufficient time for students to frame their responses. The length and quality of students' responses often track the length of time teachers are willing to wait for answers before they repeat or rephrase their questions, ask the same questions of other students, or ask other questions.

- Ask clear, precise questions. A student who does not understand what you are asking risks responding incorrectly or inappropriately and may then feel frustrated and ashamed. The next time, he or she may be reluctant to respond. A student who responds correctly or appropriately will want to try again.

- Avoid questions that may be answered with a simple Yes or No. Do not ask, for example, "Does the queen bee enjoy her position in the beehive?" Rather, ask, "Why does the queen bee say that being a bee is a joy?"

- Do not ask conformity questions, that is, questions to which students are likely to give the answers they think you expect of them rather than what they feel or think is true. Do not, for example, ask "Would you feel sad if, like the mayfly, you had only a day in which to live?" Or, "Should parents always show their love for their children?"

- Never ridicule a student who answers incorrectly or incompletely. A single mocking or sarcastic remark can do irreparable harm. Instead build upon the students' responses to draw out better answers, as in the following example:

Teacher: "Why does the worker bee say that being a bee is a pain?" [Pause] "Melinda."

Melinda: "Because he's jealous of the queen bee?"

Teacher: "I wouldn't be surprised if the worker bee is jealous of the queen bee. Why might the worker bee feel that way?" [Pause] "Melinda."

Melinda: "Well, the queen has an easy life. She gets waited on by all the other bees."

Teacher: "That's right. The queen bee's life appears to be easy. What about the worker bee's life?

Melinda: "It's a lot harder. The worker has to get up early and take out the trash and work all the time."

Teacher: "Very good, Melinda. The worker bee feels that all there is to life is hard work. And perhaps the worker is jealous of the queen. That's why the worker bee says that being a bee is a pain."

When students appear hesitant to engage in discussion or to lack the linguistic skills to express themselves orally, you may sometimes stimulate discussion by using activities in other domains that draw on other intelligences the students possess, such as assembling objects or constructing models, drawing, role-playing, and pantomime.

Drawing

Not all students are responsive to discussion, and some students may be more willing to converse at some times than at others. When child psychiatrist Robert Coles undertook his landmark study of how young children came to terms with the political and social changes in the South in the late 1950s and early 1960s, he quickly learned that he was not always able to talk with the young children he studied.

> Young children…are often uninterested in conversation. They want to be on the move, and they are often bored at the prospect of hearing words and being expected to use them. It is not that they don't have ideas and feelings, or a need to express them to others. Indeed, their games and play, their drawings and finger paintings are full of energetic symbolization and communication. It is simply that—as one eight-year-old boy once told me—"Talking is okay, but I don't like to do it all the time the way grown-ups do; I guess you have to develop the habit."*

To overcome his subjects' reluctance to talk, Coles often provided them with crayons and paints so they could express their feelings to him in their drawings and paintings. He found that even those children who initially were reluctant to draw for him invariably changed their minds.

Drawing is one of the best tools available in teaching and understanding children from the time they are quite young through adolescence. It permits them to make use of their spatial and bodily-kinesthetic intelligences, which in many cases may be more highly developed than their linguistic intelligence.

In their drawings children reveal themselves to others and to themselves. They put on paper what they know and feel about reality. In fact, drawing provides children with an initial means of gaining control of their feelings about the realities they perceive. What adults may mistake as a poor drawing may in fact be an excellent representation of the child's deeply felt reality.

These suggestions may contribute to successful use of drawing in the classroom:

- Provide your students with a variety of drawing materials. Many students will like felt-tip markers in many colors, but some may prefer crayons, water colors, or oil pastels.

- Make sure the students have ample work space. If they sit too closely together, they may be distracted or may begin copying one another's ideas.

- Set the stage for the drawing. For example, if you ask students to draw or paint a picture of fireflies sending their messages, invite the students to reflect for a few moments, as in the following example:

Teacher: "Let's close our eyes and imagine fireflies flitting about on a dark night….Think about how they glimmer and glow in the dark….Imagine them writing their vanishing messages on the darkness about them….What is it they say?…What do their glowing signs mean?…Now let's draw our pictures of fireflies, scribbling as they fly…using light to paint their nighttime pictures."

- Allow ample time for students to complete their drawings. Never give them pictures to copy.

- When your students have completed their drawings, approve what they have done. Talk about their drawings with them, showing genuine interest in their work. Give as much individual attention as you can. Ask concrete questions about what they have drawn.

- Never ridicule a student's drawing or tell a student that what he or she has drawn does not look real. Nothing will impair a student's ability to draw more than adult ridicule or interference. If a drawing has been done hurriedly or superficially, however, disapprove of it with a simple remark: "You can do better than that. Please do it over again." Or, "Please do it again—seriously this time. You have all the time you need to do it well."

- If a student is not satisfied with a drawing he or she has completed, suggest that the drawing be done again on a new sheet of paper or a new activity sheet.

Pantomime

Pantomime is the art of silent communication, of conveying ideas, feelings, experiences through bodily movements and expression, without using words. It demands concentration, sharpens perception, and stimulates the imagination. Many children enjoy pantomime, finding it a natural means of expression. It permits them to draw upon their bodily-kinesthetic intelligence, to use their entire bodies to communicate and to express what they mean or feel, clearly and artis-

---

* Robert Coles, *Children of Crisis, A Study of Courage and Fear* (Boston: Little, Brown, 1964), p. 41.

tically, even when they cannot find the words to do so.

Pantomime may be particularly effective with students whose command of English is limited or who have speech-related disabilities. Used properly, however, pantomime does not substitute for oral or written language but promotes it. Students who succeed in communicating through bodily movement increase their self-confidence and are encouraged to express themselves orally and in writing.

Here are suggestions for effective use of pantomime in the classroom:

- Approach pantomime as a means of *communication,* not as a guessing game. When students watch other students mime, do not ask the audience to guess what the players intend. Instead, ask them, "What did you see?" Do not imply that there are right or wrong answers to the question.

- Divide your class into manageable groups—no more than 15–20 in a group—so you can give participants the individual attention and opportunities they require. If your class is large, consider having half the class participate in pantomime while the other half participates in some other activity.

- Limit pantomime sessions to 10–15 minutes if you find the students are unable to sustain their attention and enthusiasm for longer periods.

- Conduct pantomime sessions in a large space; encourage the student mimes to range over the whole classroom, if the space is available. If you work with students in a larger space, such as an auditorium, however, establish clear boundaries within which students may move.

- Arrange the students so all of them may easily see and be seen, hear and be heard. Seating them on the floor in a semicircle may be the most satisfactory arrangement.

- Keep the area in which students perform and watch pantomime uncluttered.

Cooperative Games

Games used in nurturing the intelligences of students should free students from the pressure to win, which they often encounter on the playing field, and from the need to quantify or rank their performances. In fact, adults seem far more preoccupied with counting and measuring achievement in games than do children, who generally are more interested in enjoyment.

The games suggested for use in this teaching guide are cooperative rather than competitive games. They encourage students to play *with* rather than *against* each other in order to achieve common, mutually desirable goals. They are intended to help students develop their motor skills (bodily-kinesthetic intelligence) *and* their social skills (interpersonal intelligence) and to strengthen their self-concepts (intrapersonal intelligence).

Effective cooperative games are characterized by the following qualities:

- Challenges are appropriate to the ages and abilities of the players.

- Rules are minimal and easy to understand.

- Everyone who chooses to play is involved in the action.

- Players regard each other as teammates, not rivals.

- Everyone wins and no one is permitted to fail.

- Cooperation is considered an end in itself, not merely a means to victory.

- Little or no equipment or expenditure of money is required.

Teaching Poetry to Children

Former United States poet laureate and Librarian of Congress Archibald Macleish recounts a story told of an encounter between Nobel Prize-winning physicist Paul A. M. Dirac and his younger colleague Robert Oppenheimer. One day Dirac walked into his laboratory and spotted Oppenheimer, recently graduated from Harvard, among his apprentices. "So," Dirac said, "I understand you combine the writing of poetry with the study of physics." When Oppenheimer acknowledged that he did, Dirac continued, "I simply don't understand it. In science you try to say what nobody has known before in such a way that everybody will understand it, whereas in poetry...." With that, he turned and walked out to a chorus of approving laughter.

Macleish does not record any rejoinder on the part of Oppenheimer, but, more than a hundred years earlier, the English poet Percy Bysshe Shelley had aptly responded to such evaluations of poetry. Only the poet, he declared, can "... lift the veil from the hidden beauties of the world and make familiar objects be as if they were not familiar."

In 1969 American poet Kenneth Koch began seeking to help New York City schoolchildren uncover the hidden wonders of the familiar world by teaching them poetry. He had observed innovative ways of teaching art to children at New York's Metropolitan Museum and was impressed with how much children enjoyed making drawings, paintings, and collages. But children's poetry, he found, lacked the creative energy of children's art—it often was uneasily imitative of adult poetry or was childishly cute. On the other hand, he was struck by the playfulness and inventiveness of children's talk and was curious to see whether he could take advantage of their fresh and surprising ways of saying things to help them create poetry.

Koch wrote about his efforts in a book he titled *Wishes, Lies and Dreams: Teaching Children to Write Poetry*. After the book's appearance, he expanded his efforts to help children appreciate poetry by seeking ways to help them read and enjoy great poetry by adults. His work resulted in a second book, *Rose, Where Did You Get That Red? Teaching Great Poetry to Children*. The latest edition of this book includes information based on Koch's experiences of teaching poetry and poetry writing to children in other countries and in different languages, specifically in Haiti, France, Italy, and China.

Although Koch did not intend his books to provide recipes for teaching children poetry, several useful suggestions may be drawn from his writing. His suggestions have influenced the design of this literature teaching guide, and many of the poetry writing techniques he recommends also are recommended in the guide.

- Begin the teaching of poetry with writing alone. Give children an opportunity to write their own poems independently of the study of adult poems. Allow them to feel like poets, to use the sounds and meanings of words the way poets do, so they may approach the poetry of adults on somewhat equal footing with the adult poets.

- Teach reading poetry and writing poetry as one subject by giving children "poetry ideas," that is, suggestions for writing poetry of their own in some way similar to the poems they are studying. Such ideas can give children a way to experience, through writing, some of the principal ideas and feelings expressed in the poetry they are reading. The ideas should be easy to understand— neither too general ("Write a poem of your own about an insect") nor too specific ("Write a poem in which you tell how boring the life of a worker bee is"). They should

excite the children and help them think of what they want to write ("Write a poem about how it must feel to be able to walk on water like a water strider" or "Write a poem about what you would do if you could communicate like a firefly by signaling with flashes of light").

- Encourage children to write in their own language. Do not focus on the mechanical elements of writing. Do not, for example, require children to use rhyme; generally they will not be able to use it skillfully enough to create good poetry. Do not require them to spell words correctly or to present their initial work neatly; such elements can be taught or corrected later. Do not require students, at least initially, to learn sometime confusing rhetorical terms. Point out such terms—*alliteration, onomatopoeia, simile,* etc.—only after the students have become comfortable writing their poetry.

- Foster a free and inspiring classroom atmosphere conducive to poetry. Allow the students to make some noise, to read each other's lines, to walk around the room a bit, to spell words as best they can, without worrying about it.

- Read the children's poems aloud in class or allow them to do so. Photocopy or otherwise duplicate their poems and publish them in booklets along with the poems they are studying.

- Be positive; respond appreciatively to what the children say and what they write. Respond more enthusiastically to lines or ideas you particularly like rather than criticize those you like less.

- In deciding on poems to teach children, do not be put off by words unfamiliar to them, by allusions to things unknown to them, or by difficult syntax. Children are quite willing to learn new words or concepts to play new games or to understand technology-oriented films or television shows. So, too, will they be willing to do so to engage in poetry, which, if properly taught, takes on the atmosphere of a game.

Readers of Paul Fleischman's poems will note that the poet sometimes anthropomorphizes his insect subjects. That, of course, is his prerogative as a poet. Teachers who find jarring the juxtaposition of language-based activities that draw from such poems and scientific activities drawn from the same poems should feel free to separate such activities by a reasonable interval of time.

Recommended Reading

Anderson, Richard C., Elfreida H. Hiebert, Judith A. Scott, and Ian A.G. Wilkinson. *Becoming a Nation of Readers: The Report of the Commission on Reading.* Washington: The National Institute of Education, 1984.

Bettelheim, Bruno and Karen Zelan. *On Learning to Read: The Child's Fascination with Meaning.* New York: Knopf, 1982.

Brookes, Mona. *Drawing with Children: A Creative Teaching and Learning Method That Works for Adults, Too.* Los Angeles: Jeremy Tarcher, 1986.

Coles, Robert. *Children of Crisis: A Study of Courage and Fear.* Boston: Little, Brown, 1967. See Chapter 3, "When I Draw the Lord He'll Be a Real Big Man," pp. 37–71, in which Coles discusses what can be learned from children's' artistic productions.

Farnham-Diggory, Sylvia. *Schooling.* Cambridge, MA: Harvard University Press, 1990.

Garrett, Judi. *Learning Through Mime/Creative Dramatics.* Los Angeles: Performing Tree, 1981.

Johnson, David W., Roger T. Johnson, and Edythe Johnson Holubec. *Circles of Learning: Cooperation in the Classroom.* Edina, MN: Interaction Book, 1990.

Johnson, David W. and Roger T. Johnson. *Learning Together and Alone: Cooperative, Competitive, and Individualistic Learning,* 2d ed. Englewood Cliffs, NJ: Prentice Hall, 1987.

Koch, Kenneth. *Rose, Where Did You Get That Red? Teaching Great Poetry to Children.* New York: Vintage, 1990.

Koch, Kenneth and the Students of P. S. 61 in New York City. *Wishes, Lies and Dreams: Teaching Children to Write Poetry.* New York: Harper & Row, 1970.

Kohn, Alfie. *No Contest.* Boston: Houghton Mifflin, 1986. See Chapter 4: "Is Competition More Enjoyable?" pp. 79–95.

McCaslin, Nellie. *Creative Drama in the Classroom.* New York: Longman, 1984. See Chapter 4: "Pantomime: The Next Step," pp. 64–117.

Orlick, Terry. *The Cooperative Sports and Games Book.* New York: Pantheon, 1978.

———. *The Second Cooperative Sports and Games Book.* New York: Pantheon, 1982.

Sobel, Jeffrey. *Everybody Wins.* New York: Walker, 1982.

Teaching Guide Overview

For each of the teaching activities suggested for the poems of *Joyful Noise: Poems for Two Voices,* the following overview indicates

- the traditional school subject area from which the activity is drawn.

- the intelligences or blend of intellectual competences the activity may help students develop.

Introduction: Before the Reading

Suggested Teaching Activity	Subject Area	Intelligence to Be Developed
1. A Collaborative Poem	Language Arts	Linguistic; Interpersonal; Intrapersonal
2. An "I Wish" Poem	Language Arts	Linguistic; Interpersonal; Intrapersonal
3. A Comparison Poem	Language Arts	Linguistic; Interpersonal; Intrapersonal
4. A Noise Poem	Language Arts	Linguistic; Interpersonal; Intrapersonal
5. A Lie Poem	Language Arts	Linguistic; Interpersonal; Intrapersonal
6. A Color Poem	Language Arts	Linguistic; Spatial; Interpersonal; Intrapersonal
7. A Music Poem	Language Arts	Linguistic; Musical; Interpersonal; Intrapersonal
8. Other Poetry Ideas	Language Arts	Linguistic; Interpersonal; Intrapersonal

"Grasshoppers": Before the Reading

Suggested Teaching Activity	Subject Area	Intelligence to Be Developed
1. Synonyms for *Jump*	Language Arts	Linguistic; Bodily-Kinesthetic
2. Signs of the Seasons	Language Arts; Science	Linguistic; Logical-Mathematical
3. Introducing *Joyful Noise*	Language Arts	Linguistic; Logical-Mathematical

During the Reading

Suggested Teaching Activity	Subject Area	Intelligence to Be Developed
1. Initial Presentation of the Poem	Language Arts	Linguistic
2. Second Presentation of the Poem	Language Arts	Linguistic; Interpersonal
3. Student Reading of the Poem	Language Arts; Performing Arts	Linguistic; Interpersonal
4. Students' Personal Dictionaries	Language Arts	Linguistic; Interpersonal

After the Reading

Suggested Teaching Activity	Subject Area	Intelligence to Be Developed
1. Poetry Idea: "I Am a High Jumper…"	Language Arts	Linguistic; Spatial; Intrapersonal; Interpersonal
2. What Do You Know About Grasshoppers?	Science; Language Arts; Visual Arts; Computer Education	Logical-Mathematical; Linguistic; Spatial; Bodily-Kinesthetic; Interpersonal; Intrapersonal
3. Jump Like a Grasshopper	Mathematics; Physical Education	Logical-Mathematical; Linguistic; Bodily-Kinesthetic; Interpersonal
4. The Grasshopper Chorus	Science; Performing Arts	Linguistic; Musical; Bodily-Kinesthetic; Interpersonal

"Water Striders": Before the Reading

Suggested Teaching Activity	Subject Area	Intelligence to Be Developed
1. Dreams and Fantasies	Language Arts	Linguistic; Interpersonal; Intrapersonal
2. Teaching and Learning	Language Arts; Science	Linguistic; Intrapersonal; Interpersonal

During the Reading

Suggested Teaching Activity	Subject Area	Intelligence to Be Developed
1. Initial Presentation of the Poem	Language Arts	Linguistic
2. Second Presentation of the Poem	Language Arts	Linguistic; Interpersonal
3. Student Reading of the Poem	Language Arts; Performing Arts	Linguistic; Interpersonal
4. Students' Personal Dictionaries	Language Arts	Linguistic; Interpersonal

After the Reading

Suggested Teaching Activity	Subject Area	Intelligence to Be Developed
1. Poetry Idea: "If I Could…I Would"	Language Arts	Linguistic; Intrapersonal; Interpersonal
2. What Do You Know About Water Striders?	Science; Language Arts; Visual Arts; Computer Education	Logical-Mathematical; Linguistic; Spatial; Bodily-Kinesthetic; Interpersonal; Intrapersonal
3. Balderdash!	Language Arts	Linguistic; Interpersonal
4. Surface Tension	Science	Logical-Mathematical; Bodily-Kinesthetic; Linguistic
5. Pantomime	Performing Arts	Bodily-Kinesthetic; Interpersonal

"Mayflies": Before the Reading

Suggested Teaching Activity	Subject Area	Intelligence to Be Developed
1. One Day to Live	Language Arts	Linguistic; Intrapersonal; Interpersonal
2. Relativity	Language Arts	Linguistic; Logical-Mathematical; Interpersonal

During the Reading

Suggested Teaching Activity	Subject Area	Intelligence to Be Developed
1. Initial Presentation of the Poem	Language Arts	Linguistic
2. Second Presentation of the Poem	Language Arts	Linguistic; Interpersonal
3. Student Reading of the Poem	Language Arts; Performing Arts	Linguistic; Interpersonal
4. Students' Personal Dictionaries	Language Arts	Linguistic; Interpersonal

After the Reading

Suggested Teaching Activity	Subject Area	Intelligence to Be Developed
1. Poetry Idea: "If I Had Only a Day to Live…"	Language Arts	Linguistic; Intrapersonal; Interpersonal
2. What Do You Know About Mayflies?	Science; Language Arts; Visual Arts; Computer Education	Logical-Mathematical; Linguistic; Spatial; Bodily-Kinesthetic; Interpersonal; Intrapersonal
3. Hurry! Hurry!	Physical Education	Bodily-Kinesthetic; Interpersonal
4. Comparisons	Language Arts	Linguistic; Intrapersonal; Interpersonal

"Fireflies": Before the Reading

Suggested Teaching Activity	Subject Area	Intelligence to Be Developed
1. Signaling	Language Arts	Linguistic; Bodily-Kinesthetic; Interpersonal
2. Light Show	Language Arts	Linguistic; Interpersonal

During the Reading

Suggested Teaching Activity	Subject Area	Intelligence to Be Developed
1. Initial Presentation of the Poem	Language Arts	Linguistic
2. Second Presentation of the Poem	Language Arts	Linguistic; Interpersonal
3. Student Reading of the Poem	Language Arts; Performing Arts	Linguistic; Interpersonal
4. Students' Personal Dictionaries	Language Arts	Linguistic; Interpersonal

After the Reading

Suggested Teaching Activity	Subject Area	Intelligence to Be Developed
1. Poetry Idea: "I Am the Magical Messenger…"	Language Arts	Linguistic; Intrapersonal; Interpersonal
2. What Do You Know About Fireflies?	Science; Language Arts; Visual Arts; Computer Education	Logical-Mathematical; Linguistic; Spatial; Bodily-Kinesthetic; Interpersonal; Intrapersonal
3. Same Sound	Language Arts	Linguistic; Interpersonal
4. Secret Messages	Science; Language Arts	Logical-Mathematical; Linguistic; Interpersonal
5. Take a Message	Physical Education; Language Arts	Bodily-Kinesthetic; Linguistic

"Book Lice": Before the Reading

Suggested Teaching Activity	Subject Area	Intelligence to Be Developed
1. A Matter of Taste	Language Arts	Linguistic; Interpersonal
2. Opposites Attract	Language Arts	Linguistic; Interpersonal

During the Reading

Suggested Teaching Activity	Subject Area	Intelligence to Be Developed
1. Initial Presentation of the Poem	Language Arts	Linguistic
2. Second Presentation of the Poem	Language Arts	Linguistic; Interpersonal
3. Student Reading of the Poem	Language Arts; Performing Arts	Linguistic; Interpersonal
4. Students' Personal Dictionaries	Language Arts	Linguistic; Interpersonal

After the Reading

Suggested Teaching Activity	Subject Area	Intelligence to Be Developed
1. Poetry Idea: "Opposites"	Language Arts	Linguistic; Intrapersonal; Interpersonal
2. What Do You Know About Book Lice?	Science; Language Arts; Visual Arts; Computer Education	Logical-Mathematical; Linguistic; Spatial; Bodily-Kinesthetic; Interpersonal; Intrapersonal
3. Playing Favorites	Language Arts	Linguistic; Intrapersonal; Interpersonal

"The Moth's Serenade": Before the Reading

Suggested Teaching Activity	Subject Area	Intelligence to Be Developed
1. Irresistible	Language Arts	Linguistic; Interpersonal
2. Serenade	Language Arts; Performing Arts	Musical; Linguistic; Interpersonal

During the Reading

Suggested Teaching Activity	Subject Area	Intelligence to Be Developed
1. Initial Presentation of the Poem	Language Arts	Linguistic
2. Second Presentation of the Poem	Language Arts	Linguistic; Interpersonal
3. Student Reading of the Poem	Language Arts; Performing Arts	Linguistic; Interpersonal
4. Students' Personal Dictionaries	Language Arts	Linguistic; Interpersonal

After the Reading

Suggested Teaching Activity	Subject Area	Intelligence to Be Developed
1. Poetry Idea: A Metaphor Poem	Language Arts	Linguistic; Intrapersonal; Interpersonal
2. What Do You Know About Moths?	Science; Language Arts; Visual Arts; Computer Education	Logical-Mathematical; Linguistic; Spatial; Bodily-Kinesthetic; Interpersonal; Intrapersonal
3. The Compass Needle's North	Science; Social Studies	Logical-Mathematical; Bodily-Kinesthetic; Linguistic; Interpersonal
4. Circling Moths	Physical Education	Bodily-Kinesthetic; Interpersonal

"Water Boatmen": Before the Reading

Suggested Teaching Activity	Subject Area	Intelligence to Be Developed
1. Vigorous Activity	Language Arts	Linguistic; Intrapersonal; Interpersonal
2. Racing Shells	Language Arts	Linguistic; Interpersonal

During the Reading

Suggested Teaching Activity	Subject Area	Intelligence to Be Developed
1. Initial Presentation of the Poem	Language Arts	Linguistic
2. Second Presentation of the Poem	Language Arts	Linguistic; Interpersonal
3. Student Reading of the Poem	Language Arts; Performing Arts	Linguistic; Interpersonal
4. Students' Personal Dictionaries	Language Arts	Linguistic; Interpersonal

After the Reading

Suggested Teaching Activity	Subject Area	Intelligence to Be Developed
1. Poetry Idea: Animal Movement	Language Arts	Linguistic; Intrapersonal; Interpersonal
2. What Do You Know About Water Boatmen?	Science; Language Arts; Visual Arts; Computer Education	Logical-Mathematical; Linguistic; Spatial; Bodily-Kinesthetic; Interpersonal; Intrapersonal
3. Teamwork	Physical Education	Bodily Kinesthetic; Linguistic; Interpersonal
4. I've Got Rhythm	Performing Arts; Language Arts	Bodily-Kinesthetic; Musical; Linguistic; Interpersonal

"The Digger Wasp": Before the Reading

Suggested Teaching Activity	Subject Area	Intelligence to Be Developed
1. Talk Is Cheap	Language Arts	Linguistic; Logical-Mathematical; Intrapersonal; Interpersonal
2. Showing Care	Language Arts	Linguistic; Intrapersonal; Interpersonal

During the Reading

Suggested Teaching Activity	Subject Area	Intelligence to Be Developed
1. Initial Presentation of the Poem	Language Arts	Linguistic
2. Second Presentation of the Poem	Language Arts	Linguistic; Interpersonal
3. Student Reading of the Poem	Language Arts; Performing Arts	Linguistic; Interpersonal
4. Students' Personal Dictionaries	Language Arts	Linguistic; Interpersonal

After the Reading

Suggested Teaching Activity	Subject Area	Intelligence to Be Developed
1. Poetry Idea: "Caring Means…"	Language Arts	Linguistic; Intrapersonal; Interpersonal
2. What Do You Know About Digger Wasps?	Science; Language Arts; Visual Arts; Computer Education	Logical-Mathematical; Linguistic; Spatial; Bodily-Kinesthetic; Interpersonal; Intrapersonal
3. Safe and Snug	Visual Arts	Spatial; Bodily-Kinesthetic; Linguistic; Intrapersonal; Interpersonal
4. Advice for the Future	Language Arts	Linguistic; Intrapersonal; Interpersonal
5. Knots and Tangles	Physical Education	Bodily-Kinesthetic; Linguistic; Logical-Mathematical

"Cicadas": Before the Reading

Suggested Teaching Activity	Subject Area	Intelligence to Be Developed
1. Choral and Solo Singing	Performing Arts	Musical; Linguistic; Intrapersonal; Interpersonal
2. Better Weather	Language Arts	Linguistic; Intrapersonal; Interpersonal

During the Reading

Suggested Teaching Activity	Subject Area	Intelligence to Be Developed
1. Initial Presentation of the Poem	Language Arts	Linguistic
2. Second Presentation of the Poem	Language Arts	Linguistic; Interpersonal
3. Student Reading of the Poem	Language Arts; Performing Arts	Linguistic; Interpersonal
4. Students' Personal Dictionaries	Language Arts	Linguistic; Interpersonal

After the Reading

Suggested Teaching Activity	Subject Area	Intelligence to Be Developed
1. Poetic Devices	Language Arts	Linguistic; Logical-Mathematical; Interpersonal
2. Poetry Idea: Joyful Noises	Language Arts	Linguistic; Intrapersonal; Interpersonal
3. What Do You Know About Cicadas?	Science; Language Arts; Visual Arts; Computer Education	Logical-Mathematical; Linguistic; Spatial; Bodily-Kinesthetic; Interpersonal; Intrapersonal
4. Taking a Sound Field Trip	Language Arts; Performing Arts	Logical-Mathematical; Musical; Linguistic; Intrapersonal; Interpersonal
5. A Joyful Mood	Visual Arts; Performing Arts	Spatial; Bodily-Kinesthetic; Musical; Linguistic; Interpersonal
6. How Is Sound Produced?	Science; Performing Arts	Logical-Mathematical; Musical; Interpersonal; Linguistic

"Honeybees": Before the Reading

Suggested Teaching Activity	Subject Area	Intelligence to Be Developed
1. Associations and Groups	Language Arts	Linguistic; Logical-Mathematical; Intrapersonal; Interpersonal
2. Different Points of View	Language Arts	Linguistic; Intrapersonal; Interpersonal

During the Reading

Suggested Teaching Activity	Subject Area	Intelligence to Be Developed
1. Initial Presentation of the Poem	Language Arts	Linguistic
2. Second Presentation of the Poem	Language Arts	Linguistic; Interpersonal
3. Student Reading of the Poem	Language Arts; Performing Arts	Linguistic; Interpersonal
4. Students' Personal Dictionaries	Language Arts	Linguistic; Interpersonal

After the Reading

Suggested Teaching Activity	Subject Area	Intelligence to Be Developed
1. Poetry Idea: Points of View	Language Arts	Linguistic; Intrapersonal; Interpersonal
2. What Do You Know About Honeybees?	Science; Language Arts; Visual Arts; Computer Education	Logical-Mathematical; Linguistic; Spatial; Bodily-Kinesthetic; Interpersonal; Intrapersonal
3. Active and Passive	Language Arts	Linguistic; Interpersonal
4. Strength in Numbers	Physical Education	Linguistic; Logical-Mathematical; Bodily-Kinesthetic; Intrapersonal; Interpersonal

"Whirligig Beetles": Before the Reading

Suggested Teaching Activity	Subject Area	Intelligence to Be Developed
1. The Enjoyment of Traveling	Language Arts	Linguistic; Intrapersonal; Interpersonal
2. Shortest Distance/ Best Distance	Language Arts	Logical-Mathematical; Linguistic; Intrapersonal; Interpersonal

During the Reading

Suggested Teaching Activity	Subject Area	Intelligence to Be Developed
1. Initial Presentation of the Poem	Language Arts	Linguistic
2. Second Presentation of the Poem	Language Arts	Linguistic; Interpersonal
3. Student Reading of the Poem	Language Arts; Performing Arts	Linguistic; Interpersonal
4. Students' Personal Dictionaries	Language Arts	Linguistic; Interpersonal

After the Reading

Suggested Teaching Activity	Subject Area	Intelligence to Be Developed
1. What Do You Know About Whirligig Beetles?	Science; Language Arts; Visual Arts; Computer Education	Logical-Mathematical; Linguistic; Spatial; Bodily-Kinesthetic; Interpersonal; Intrapersonal
2. Poetry Idea: "Eyes in the Back of My Head"	Language Arts	Linguistic; Spatial; Intrapersonal; Interpersonal
3. Circles, Spirals, Arcs, Ovals, and Loops	Mathematics; Visual Arts	Spatial; Logical-Mathematical; Linguistic; Interpersonal
4. Dance, Dance, Dance	Performing Arts	Bodily-Kinesthetic; Musical; Linguistic; Intrapersonal; Interpersonal
5. Whirligiging	Physical Education	Bodily-Kinesthetic; Spatial; Linguistic

"Requiem": Before the Reading

Suggested Teaching Activity	Subject Area	Intelligence to Be Developed
1. Grant Them Rest	Performing Arts	Musical; Linguistic; Intrapersonal; Interpersonal
2. Memorial Service	Language Arts	Linguistic; Intrapersonal; Interpersonal

During the Reading

Suggested Teaching Activity	Subject Area	Intelligence to Be Developed
1. Initial Presentation of the Poem	Language Arts	Linguistic
2. Second Presentation of the Poem	Language Arts	Linguistic; Interpersonal
3. Student Reading of the Poem	Language Arts; Performing Arts	Linguistic; Interpersonal
4. Students' Personal Dictionaries	Language Arts	Linguistic; Interpersonal

After the Reading

Suggested Teaching Activity	Subject Area	Intelligence to Be Developed
1. Poetry Idea: Eulogy	Language Arts	Linguistic; Intrapersonal; Interpersonal
2. What Do You Know About Mantises, Darners, Damselflies, and Katydids?	Science; Language Arts; Visual Arts; Computer Education	Logical-Mathematical; Linguistic; Spatial; Bodily-Kinesthetic; Interpersonal; Intrapersonal
3. What Color Do You Feel?	Visual Arts	Spatial; Bodily-Kinesthetic; Linguistic; Intrapersonal; Interpersonal

"House Crickets": Before the Reading

Suggested Teaching Activity	Subject Area	Intelligence to Be Developed
1. Favorite Seasons	Language Arts	Linguistic; Intrapersonal; Interpersonal
2. Favorite Foods	Language Arts	Linguistic; Intrapersonal; Interpersonal

During the Reading

Suggested Teaching Activity	Subject Area	Intelligence to Be Developed
1. Initial Presentation of the Poem	Language Arts	Linguistic
2. Second Presentation of the Poem	Language Arts	Linguistic; Interpersonal
3. Student Reading of the Poem	Language Arts; Performing Arts	Linguistic; Interpersonal
4. Students' Personal Dictionaries	Language Arts	Linguistic; Interpersonal

After the Reading

Suggested Teaching Activity	Subject Area	Intelligence to Be Developed
1. Poetry Idea: Change of Seasons	Language Arts	Linguistic; Intrapersonal; Interpersonal
2. What Do You Know About House Crickets?	Science; Language Arts; Visual Arts; Computer Education	Logical-Mathematical; Linguistic; Spatial; Bodily-Kinesthetic; Interpersonal; Intrapersonal
3. Temperature Conversions	Science; Mathematics	Logical-Mathematical; Linguistic; Interpersonal
4. Sounds Like…	Language Arts	Linguistic; Logical-Mathematical; Interpersonal

"Chrysalis Diary": Before the Reading

Suggested Teaching Activity	Subject Area	Intelligence to Be Developed
1. Change	Language Arts	Linguistic; Intrapersonal; Logical-Mathematical; Interpersonal
2. Diaries	Language Arts	Linguistic; Intrapersonal; Interpersonal

During the Reading

Suggested Teaching Activity	Subject Area	Intelligence to Be Developed
1. Initial Presentation of the Poem	Language Arts	Linguistic
2. Second Presentation of the Poem	Language Arts	Linguistic; Interpersonal
3. Student Reading of the Poem	Language Arts; Performing Arts	Linguistic; Interpersonal
4. Students' Personal Dictionaries	Language Arts	Linguistic; Interpersonal

After the Reading

Suggested Teaching Activity	Subject Area	Intelligence to Be Developed
1. Poetry Idea: A Diary Poem	Language Arts	Linguistic; Intrapersonal; Interpersonal
2. What Do You Know About Butterflies?	Science; Language Arts; Visual Arts; Computer Education	Logical-Mathematical; Linguistic; Spatial; Bodily-Kinesthetic; Interpersonal; Intrapersonal
3. Organizing and Retrieving Information	Computer Education	Logical-Mathematical; Linguistic; Interpersonal
4. Class Books	Visual Arts; Language Arts; Computer Education	Spatial; Linguistic; Logical-Mathematical; Interpersonal; Intrapersonal
5. Word Games	Language Arts	Linguistic; Interpersonal

Joyful Noise
Poems for Two Voices

by Paul Fleischman
Illustrated by Eric Beddows

INTRODUCTION

Before the Reading

In *Joyful Noise: Poems for Two Voices,* Paul Fleischman lifts the veil from the hidden wonders of the familiar world of insects. His imaginative poems are a delight to the ear, as his collaborator Eric Beddows' illustrations are a delight for the eye.

Before introducing your students to Fleischman's poems, give them opportunities to write their own poems, independent of those they will be reading. Doing so will give the students a chance to feel like poets and will make poetry less intimidating to them than it otherwise might be. Then, when they take up the poems in *Joyful Noise* and subsequently attempt to write poems inspired by Fleischman's work, they will have had the experience of using poetry's tools and materials. They will already know what it is like to write poetry. This approach also will give you a sense of what your students like about poetry and of how you might best help them write it and enjoy it.

Here are some poetry writing suggestions to help you prepare your students to read *Joyful Noise* with understanding and enjoyment. The suggestions are based on poetry writing activities developed by poet Kenneth Koch as he taught schoolchildren how to write poetry and to appreciate poetry written by others. They may take several class periods to complete, but it will be time well spent.

1. A Collaborative Poem. Begin by inviting all of the students in class to collaborate in creating a poem. Explain that each student will write one line of the poem on a piece of paper and turn it in and that you will read all of their lines as a single poem.

Tell the students that no one should put his or her name on the line he or she contributes. In this way no student has to be anxious about not being able to write a good poem, since each is responsible for writing only one line, and no one has to worry about how his or her poem is evaluated in relation to someone else's.

To give the final poem unity, suggest some rules that each writer should follow regarding what should be included in their lines. You might, for example, propose that every line begin with "I wish" or " I hope" and then ask students to suggest other rules. When Kenneth Koch first attempted a collaborative poem with his students in a New York public school, the students decided that every line should contain a color, a comic strip character, and a city or state, and should begin with the words "I wish."

Circulate among the students as they write their lines and offer assistance and encouragement as needed. When the students have completed their lines, collect them, shuffle them, and read them aloud as a poem. Do not be concerned whether every line obeys all the regulations agreed on.

Ask the students to suggest names for their collaborative poem. Although their product probably will not be great poetry, it might help them feel like poets and encourage them to write more.

If students have enjoyed collaborating on their poem, invite them to try again, this time with a different set of rules about what should be included in each line. Repeat the process described above.

Materials

Writing paper; pens or pencils

2. An "I Wish" Poem. Build on the students' experience of collaboration by inviting each student individually to write an "I Wish" poem. Explain that each line of the poem should begin with the words "I wish." Tell the students that their wishes may be real or far-fetched and that their poems need not be of any particular length. Tell them not to try to use rhyme in their poems.

These instructions will provide the students with a form that will give unity to their poems and that probably will be easy for them to work with. They can begin each line afresh, without worrying about how to tie their poems together. The instructions also give students something to write about in which most, if not all, of them are truly interested: the special world of their personal wishes. And because there are no limits to what one can wish, the instructions encourage them to let their imaginations take flight.

Answer any questions the students may have about the "I Wish" poems. Offer examples, if necessary, of the kinds of lines they might write and the subjects they might deal with. You might say, for example, "You can wish you were some famous person or that you lived somewhere else or that you had special powers," or "You might wish that you could fly or that there were no wars in the world or that you were fabulously wealthy." Ask students to suggest some ideas or sample lines of their own.

When you are confident the students understand the instructions for their "I Wish" poems, encourage them to begin writing. Circulate among them as they write and offer assistance and encouragement as appropriate.

Allow the students to talk about their poems with their classmates as they write them and to look at one another's work in progress. If some students finish their poems quickly, while other students are still writing, suggest that they write another. If some students have serious difficulty writing their poems, pair them with other students with whom they can collaborate or collaborate with the students yourself.

When the students have completed their poems, collect them and read them aloud to the class. Respond appreciatively to what they have written. Respond with particular enthusiasm to writing you especially like. If a word or line of a poem is not clear, ask the student what he or she meant, but resist the temptation to correct or improve upon students' poetry.

3. A Comparison Poem. Stimulate your students to think like poets by holding up or pointing out items in their immediate environment—a pencil, a piece of paper, a book, a piece of chalk—and asking them to compare each item to something that is like it in at least one way. A pencil might be compared to a rocket or a telephone pole, a piece of chalk to a snowy day or vanilla ice cream. If the students can see the sky or a tree through a classroom window, ask them what in the classroom most resembles the sky or tree. Ask them to compare something in school with something outside of school, something big with something small, the color of their hair or eyes or a piece of clothing with something like it.

Tell the students that poets often make comparisons and that good comparisons help us see or understand things better. Invite the students to write comparison poems. Encourage them to feel free to make whatever comparisons come to their minds, no matter how unusual.

Suggest that their poems might include one comparison in every line. If necessary, to make your poetry idea clear, write the words LIKE and AS in big letters on the chalkboard and tell the students to include one of these comparisons in each line.

When you are confident the students understand the poetry idea, encourage them to begin writing. Circulate among them as they write and offer assistance and encouragement as appropriate.

As with the "I Wish" poems, allow the students to talk with their classmates as they write and to look at one another's work in progress. Encourage students who finish writing before others to write additional comparison poems. Pair students who have difficulty writing with other students with whom they can collaborate, or collaborate with these students yourself.

When the students have completed their poems, collect them and read them aloud to the class. Or invite your student poets to read their own works to the class. Respond appreciatively, showing particular enthusiasm for poems you find especially appealing or imaginative.

4. A Noise Poem. Encourage your students to think about sounds and to associate sounds with words the way a poet does. Begin by asking the students to be as quiet as they can. Then crumple a piece of paper and ask them what it sounds like (rain on the roof? eating potato chips? walking on wet pavement?). Drop keys on the floor and ask the same question. Drum your fingers on a desktop, close a door, run an eraser across the chalkboard, and ask the same question.

Next help the students associate words with sounds. Choose an onomatopoetic word—*crack, buzz, hiss*—and ask them to name other words that sound like it but whose meanings do not have anything to do with it (*track, lack, black, flack; fuzz, does, was; miss, bliss, kiss*). Make a noise—hit a chair back with a ruler, close a desk drawer, walk heavily across the classroom—and ask the students for words the noise sounds like. If necessary, have them close their eyes, listen closely to the noise again, and try to hear a word in the noise.

Once the students are thinking creatively and imaginatively about about sounds and words, tell them that poets often think in sounds, that the way words sound is important to good poetry. Invite them to write noise poems. Tell them they may write sound comparisons, in which they say what a sound is like ("The rain is like thousands of tiny drumbeats on the roof") or lines that imitate sounds ("The birds in the tree chitter-chatter").

Answer any questions the students may have about the noise poems. If necessary, offer examples of the kinds of lines they might write and ask students to suggest some ideas or sample lines of their own.

When you are confident the students understand the instructions for their noise poems, encourage them to begin writing. Circulate among them and offer assistance and encouragement.

Permit the students to talk about their poems with their classmates as they write and to share work in progress. Have students who complete their poems quickly write other noise poems. Have students who have serious difficulty writing their poems collaborate with other students or with you.

Materials

Writing paper; pens or pencils

When the students have completed their poems, collect them and read them aloud to the class or invite the students to read their poems aloud. Respond appreciatively and enthusiastically. Invite students, if necessary, to clarify what they have written, but be careful not to try to improve upon their work. Post the students' poems in the classroom for all the students and classroom visitors to read.

5. A Lie Poem. Ask a volunteer student to tell you the most outlandish lie he or she can think of. Then invite another volunteer to try to top the first student's statement with a statement even stranger and more fantastic. Continue this process, giving other students opportunities to top the previous lie. The purpose of this activity, of course, is not to promote dishonesty but to encourage the free imagining, the inventiveness, that is a hallmark of good poetry.

When the students have gotten into the spirit of unfettered imagining, tell them that good poets are able to imagine that things are different than they really are, and, in that way, help us see our world in a new way or discover things about it we might otherwise miss. Then invite the students to write lie poems. Suggest they might write something in every line of their poems that is not true, or simply make entire poems of something that is not true.

Answer any questions the students might have about their lie poems. Offer examples, if necessary, of the kinds of poems they might write and the subjects they might deal with. You might say, for example, "You can write that you have powers or abilities that you do not really have" or "You can write that you are something that you are not or that you have done something you really have not done." Ask students to suggest some ideas or sample lines of their own.

When the students understand the instructions for their lie poems, encourage them to begin writing. Circulate and offer assistance and encouragement.

Assure the students that they may share their work with their classmates as they write their poems. Encourage students who finish their poems quickly to write additional lie poems or to collaborate with the students who are having difficulty with this poetry idea.

Collect the completed poems and read them aloud to the class or have the students read their work aloud. Respond appreciatively and enthusiastically, seeking clarification as necessary. If students have enjoyed writing lie poems, invite them to compose additional poems in which they try to top their previous lies or the lies they found the most outlandish among the classmates' poems. Post the students' poems in the classroom.

6. A Color Poem. Encourage the students to associate colors with their sensations of the world around them. Ask them, for example, to look up at the sky or out at the grass or trees and see if there is anything in the classroom that is the same color. Ask them to close their eyes and to listen to various sounds: paper being crumpled, keys being dropped on the floor or jangled, hands clapping. Ask what colors the sounds are. Ask them to listen to various numbers—one, ten, a thousand—and to write down what colors the numbers are. Do the same for the names of countries, the days of the week or the seasons of the year.

Materials

Writing paper; pens or pencils

Materials

Writing paper; pens or pencils

When the students have become comfortable associating their sensations with colors, tell them that good poets often are especially skillful at helping us to recognize in objects and ideas more than what meets the eye, the ear, the touch, the taste. Then invite the students to write color poems. Tell them they might write about the colors of sounds, numbers, countries, days of the week, and so on. Suggest that they put a different color in each line of their poems. Or suggest that they might create one-color poems, in which everything in their poems is the same color or different shades of the same color.

Ask students to suggest some ideas or sample lines for color poems. When they understand the instructions for writing color poems, encourage them to begin writing. Circulate and offer assistance and encouragement.

Permit them to share their work with their classmates as they write. Students who finish their poems before others do may write additional color poems or collaborate with students who find this poetry idea difficult.

Collect the completed poems and read them aloud to the class or invite the students to read their work aloud. Respond appreciatively and enthusiastically. If they have enjoyed this poetry idea, give students opportunities to write additional color poems. Post the students' poems in the classroom.

7. A Music Poem. Encourage the students to associate music they hear with colors, places, times or seasons of the year, sounds, and feelings of happiness and sadness. Ask the students to close their eyes and listen closely as you play recordings of three or four musical selections from the classical or popular repertoires. Play each selection for at least 30 seconds and then ask the students questions about it: What colors did you see as you listened to the music? Did you see a country or city? Did you feel warm or cold? What sounds did the music remind you of?

Then tell the students you will play a new selection for them and ask them, as they listen, to write whatever the music makes them think of— their poems may be descriptions of scenes, stories, dreams, or a series of images. Almost any type of music may be used for this poetry-writing activity, including symphonic music, rock, blues, jazz, and folk.

Because students have already written poems that have a definite form, such as the wish poem, they may have ideas about how to divide their poems into lines. If some students have difficulty dividing their poems into lines, suggest that they listen to the music, write one line of their poems, listen again and write the next line, and so on.

Collect the students' completed poems and read them aloud to the class or invite the students to read their work aloud. If appropriate, as the poems are read, play in the background the musical piece that inspired them. Respond appreciatively and enthusiastically to the students' work. If they have enjoyed this poetry idea, give them opportunities to write additional music poems, using different types of music to inspire their writing. Post the students' poems in the classroom.

8. Other Poetry Ideas. If your students have been responsive to the poetry ideas you have presented and you think they will benefit from more poetry writing before they reading *Joyful Noise*, choose from among the following additional ideas:

Materials

Musical selections and appropriate playback equipment

Writing paper; pens or pencils

Materials

Writing paper; pens or pencils

- *A combination poem.* Suggest that the students write poems that combine some of the poetry ideas they have already used. For example, have them combine comparison and color poems, wish and lie poems, or noise, color, and comparison poems.

- *An "I Used To/But Now" poem.* Encourage the students to write poems that describe their own past and present, that is, poems that contrast the way they used to be and the way they are now. Suggest that they begin every odd line with "I used to," and every even line with "But now."

- *A similarity poem.* Tell the students to think about something that is *like* something else and then to imagine that it actually *is* that other thing. For example, they might think about sand on the beach being *like* brown sugar and then imagine that it *is* brown sugar. Tell them to write poems in which they describe things using *is* instead of *is like*. (For example, "The beach is covered with brown sugar.") Tell them they may write whole poems about one such comparison or may write poems that include a new comparison of this type in each line.

- *An "I Seem To Be/But Really I Am" poem.* Invite the students to write poems in which they contrast the way they seem to other people to the way they really are, that is, to the way they feel they are, deep inside themselves. Suggest that they begin every odd line with the words "I seem to be" and every even line with the words "But really I am."

- *A "What Would It Be Like?" poem.* Bring a small, tame animal, such as a mouse, a hamster or a rabbit, to the classroom. Allow each student, under supervision, to hold the animal. Then invite the students to write poems on what it would be like to be the animal, that is, to write the poem from the animal's point of view.

- *A two-student collaboration poem.* Capitalize on students' enjoyment of writing a poem with a fellow poet. Pair students and suggest several ways in which they might collaborate on a poem. Tell them they might write alternate lines of the poem, handing their paper back and forth as they complete their lines. Tell them they might write alternate lines without showing their lines to their collaborators. Thus, each student might write a line, fold the paper so his or her partner cannot see what has been written, and hand the paper to the partner, who then writes the next line, and so on. Or have each student write a series of difficult, even impossible, questions on a sheet of paper. Collect the papers and distribute them at random. Encourage the students to answer the questions they received. For some of the two-student collaboration poems, the themes already described, such as comparisons, colors, wishes, and lies, might be used to stimulate the students' imaginations or give structure to their writing.

GRASSHOPPERS

Before the Reading

Prepare your students to read Paul Fleischman's poem "Grasshoppers" by using one or both of the following suggestions:

1. Write the word *jump* in large letters on the chalkboard. Ask the students to suggest as many words as they can that mean the same thing or something similar. Write their suggestions on the chalkboard, or invite a volunteer student to do so. Elicit from the students the different shades of meaning of the words suggested. Encourage willing students to demonstrate through bodily actions the differences among the words.

Tell them that they are about to listen to a poem using many of the words they have suggested. Ask them to predict what the poem might be about.

2. Ask the students to identify signs of the changing seasons. Ask, for example, for signs by which they can tell autumn is coming (the leaves on many trees begin to change color; it gets light later in the morning and dark sooner in the evening; the temperature tends to drop; etc.). Ask the students what their favorite seasons are, and why.

Tell students they are about to read a poem that includes some signs of a change of season. Encourage them to listen carefully to determine the season.

3. Display a copy of *Joyful Noise* for the students to see. Explain that in this book Paul Fleischman's poems involve some familiar inhabitants of the world around us. Write the title of the book on the chalkboard. Then write the author's name, *Paul Fleischman,* below the title. Share what you know about Mr. Fleischman. (See "Introducing Paul Fleischman.") Below the author's name, write the name of the illustrator, *Eric Beddows.* Ask what an illustrator might be able to add to written words in a book.

Ask the students to speculate about the title of the book. Ask: Who or what makes a joyful noise? What sort of noises do you think sound joyful? What is the most joyful noise you can think of?

Materials

Copy of *Joyful Noise*

During the Reading

1. Have the students listen as you play for them a reading of "Grasshoppers" that you and a colleague have recorded on audiotape prior to the class. Alternatively, play the recording of the poem available on cassette tape from Harper & Row, publishers of *Joyful Noise*. Or, prior to class, carefully prepare to read the poem aloud along with one of your students, you taking the left-hand part and the student the right-hand part.

Set the stage for your reading or tape playback by helping your students focus their attention on the poem. Ask them to imagine what it might feel like to be able to hop, jump, and vault at will, to move effortlessly over and around obstacles.

Then play the prerecorded version of the poem or read the poem to the students. Read with appropriate expression to help the students apply their imaginations to the poem. Emphasize the exuberance, or delightful abandon, with which Fleischman's grasshoppers step out into spring, hopping, jumping, vaulting, leaping from place to place.

Materials

Teacher copy of *Joyful Noise*

Tape recorder and prerecorded version of "Grasshoppers" (optional; a cassette tape, *Joyful Noise and I Am Phoenix, Poems for Two Voices,* by Paul Fleischman, performed by John Bedford Lloyd and Anne Twomey, available from Harper & Row)

Copy of *Joyful Noise* for student reader (optional)

Materials

Student copies of *Joyful Noise*

Tape recorder and prerecorded version of "Grasshoppers" (optional)

Materials

Student copies of *Joyful Noise*

Tape recorders for student use

Materials

Notebooks students may use to create personal dictionaries

2. Distribute copies of *Joyful Noise* to the students, and have them follow in their copies as you one again play for them the prerecorded version of "Grasshoppers" or as you reread the poem with the student with whom you practiced.

Ask the students what they pictured in their minds as they listened to "Grasshoppers." If you introduced the poem by asking the students to think of synonyms for *jump*, ask how many of those words the poet used in his poem. Ask what words and phrases he used to signal that his poem would be set in springtime.

Challenge the students to determine what is similar about many of the words in the poem. Point out how many of the words end in *-er* and *-ing*. Ask whether the poet might have used such words intentionally and, if so, why.

Ask the students what Paul Fleischman thinks of grasshoppers. Ask whether his poem makes them think of grasshoppers any differently than they may have previously.

3. Allow the students to read "Grasshoppers" again, silently. Then pair students and ask each pair to practice reading the poem, or selected portions of it, together. Explain, as poet Paul Fleischman does in his introductory note, that one reader is to take the left-hand part of the poem and the other the right-hand part. Tell them that they are to read from top to bottom and that when both readers have lines on the same horizontal level, they are to speak them at the same time.

Give pairs opportunities to record and play back their readings to help them achieve a smooth presentation. Tell them that when they think they are ready, they can read the poem or a selected portion of it to the class or to a small group within the class. Or they may play back a recording they have made of their reading.

If some students have difficulty with this form of oral presentation, pair them with students more skilled at it. Assist pairs as needed, including helping them to devise means of signaling each other when to read together and when to read separately.

4. Distribute notebooks to the students in which they may create personal dictionaries of unfamiliar words they encounter in *Joyful Noise*. (See "Teaching Suggestions: Reading Strategies.") If you think it appropriate for your students, distribute to them copies of the Glossary found at the end of this unit. Tell the students that unlike a dictionary, a glossary indicates what a word or phrase means in a particular piece of writing, not all the possible meanings.

Tell the students that in the poems, they may come upon a number of words and references they do not know. Encourage them to seek from other students—reading partners, cooperative group members, and so on—suggestions about the meanings and pronunciations of words. Assure them that you will give them ideas for discovering and mastering the word meanings.

After the Reading

Materials

Writing paper; pens or pencils

Materials

Blank overhead transparency and overhead projector (optional)

Activity Sheet 1 (one per student, pair, or cooperative group)

Printed resources about insects

Pens or pencils; drawing instruments

Activity Sheet 2 (optional; one per student, pair, or cooperative group)

1. Poetry Idea: "I Am a High Jumper…" Ask the students to imagine how their movement from place to place might be different if they were able to jump and leap great distances in comparison to their size, the way a grasshopper does. Ask how they would travel around their neighborhoods and move about in school and at home.

Invite the students to write poems of their own, inspired by Paul Fleischman's "Grasshoppers." Suggest that they write poems in which they are able to jump as high or as far as they want. Tell them they might begin their poems with words such as "I am a high jumper." Suggest that they use a different word for *jump* in every line of their poems. Tell them that if they wish, they can use words that end in *-er* or in *-ing,* the way Fleischman does.

Answer any questions the students may have about this poetry idea. If necessary, offer examples of the kinds of lines they might write ("I am a high jumper/a far leaper/Bounding from place to place/Skipping over trees and houses…") and ask students to suggest some sample lines and ideas of their own.

When you are confident the students understand the instructions, encourage them to begin writing. Circulate among them and offer assistance, if needed.

Encourage the students to talk about their poems with one another and to share their work in progress. Have students who quickly complete their poems collaborate with students who are having difficulty or have them write an additional poem.

When the students have completed their poems, invite them to read them aloud to the class. Respond appreciatively, seeking clarification when necessary. Post the students' poems in the classroom. Save the poems you have posted, as possible contributions to a book of student poetry to be compiled when this poetry teaching unit has been completed.

2. What Do You Know About Grasshoppers? Ask how many students have ever seen a grasshopper. Ask those who have (surely, almost all of the students) if they can describe the grasshopper's distinguishing features: its size, color, behavior, etc.

Ask if all grasshoppers are the same or if there is more than one kind. Point out that "grasshopper" actually is a name given to several *families* of winged and wingless, heavy-bodied, jumping insects and that there actually are hundreds of different *species* of grasshopper.

Introduce students to, or review with them, the ways in which animals, including insects, are classified into categories, based on their characteristics. Sketch the taxonomy of insects on the chalkboard or display it as an overhead transparency, using grasshoppers as an example.

FOR THE TEACHER

Animals, including insects, are classified according to a hierarchy of categories, each of which contains the category below, or subordinate, to it. The principal categories include *phylum, class, order, family, genus,* and *species.*

Insects belong to the phylum *Arthropoda.* They are arthropods, which means they are invertebrates—animals with no backbones—that have a hard, protective exoskeleton, a kind of armor plating that protects its inner workings.

Insects belong to the class *Insecta*. Unlike other arthropods, including crustaceans (such as lobsters, crabs, and shrimps) or arachnids (such as spiders, scorpions, and mites), insects have three major divisions to their bodies—head, thorax, and abdomen—and only three pairs of legs, which are attached to the thorax, or second body division.

There are about 30 basic groups, or *Orders,* within the class Insecta. For example, grasshoppers are members of the order *Orthoptera.* Included in the same order are crickets and katydids. Some members of the order are winged, others are wingless. All of them have mouthparts intended for chewing and most of them feed on plants.

Within each order of insects are *Families,* which generally contain species that are similar in appearance and habits. Grasshoppers, for example, belong to the family *Acrididae.* They are jumping Orthoptera, with short antennae that customarily do not extend beyond the thoracic region, and large hearing organs, which are located on the sides of the first abdominal segment. Most adult grasshoppers have wings and many of them are strong fliers, but some species are wingless.

The two lowest rank categories of animals are *Genus* and *Species.* From these we get animals' scientific names. The first name, which is capitalized, is its generic name and the second name, not capitalized, is its specific name. Thus, one of the hundreds of species of grasshoppers is named *Melanoplus devastator,* whose common name is the "devastating grasshopper." Another is named *Trimeritropis pallidipennis,* commonly know as the pallid-winged grasshopper.

This system of naming animals was originally proposed by Carolus Linnaeus, an 18th century Swedish botanist, and is used throughout the world in its original latinized form.

Materials

Clear glass, wide-mouthed jars (optional)

10-power magnifying glass (optional)

Terrariums created of clear glass, wide-mouthed jars furnished with dirt and plants (optional)

Distribute to the students copies of Activity Sheet 1. Provide them with or guide them to resources they may use to gather information about grasshoppers so they may complete the activity sheet. (See the Recommended Reading and Audiovisual Resources and Biological Supply Houses lists at the end of the literature teaching guide. Encyclopedias and books on general biology or the life sciences may also provide information to help students complete the activity sheet.)

In addition, if time of year and location are appropriate, encourage the students to gather as much information about grasshoppers as they can simply by observing the insects in their natural habitats. Explain that careful observation generally involves only a little patience and modest tools.

Suggest that students follow the directions on Activity Sheet 2 to make sweeping nets with which they can collect grasshoppers. Suggest they also obtain clear glass, wide-mouthed jars with lids that have been punched with air holes. With a little care and quick reflexes, they may be able to capture grasshoppers in the nets and transfer them to such jars so they have an opportunity to observe the insects closely. Tell them to place twigs or weed stems in the jars to give the grasshoppers something to hold onto so they remain still. Tell them they might also find a magnifying glass (a ten-power glass is sufficient) helpful in observing the details of the grasshopper's structure and coloring. Finally, tell your students to be sure to return the grasshopper to its natural habitat when their observations have been completed.

As an adjunct or alternative to observations that individual students conduct of grasshoppers in their natural habitats, arrange for students to conduct observations in the classroom setting. Have one or more students capture grasshoppers, in the manner just described, and bring them to the classroom. (If this is not possible, order live specimens from one of the biological supply houses listed at the end of this teaching guide.) Place the grasshoppers in terrariums created by adding soil and plants to large, wide-mouthed jars placed on their sides. (Tell students to make sure the jar lids have air holes punched in them.) Encourage the students to observe and record the physical characteristics of the grasshoppers, their eating habits, and so on. Encourage them to use the grasshoppers as models for illustrations they make on their activity sheets.

Tell students they may conduct their research and field or classroom observations individually, with partners, or in small groups of three or four students. Students who work with others may divide the tasks required to complete the activity sheet, but each pair or cooperative group should be prepared to demonstrate the tasks each member performed and all students should be able to explain any of the information provided on the completed activity sheet.

When the students have completed their activity sheets, invite them to report to their classmates the information they have gathered. When information provided by students differs, have them cite their sources of information—printed materials, audiovisual resources, and field observations—and try to determine why there are differences among the reports.

Tell the students that Paul Fleischman has written some other poems about the world of insects, and they will be reading those too. Have the individual students, pairs, or cooperative groups keep the activity sheets they have prepared on grasshoppers to combine in a class publication with similar activity sheets on the other insects featured in the poems of *Joyful Noise*.

FOR THE TEACHER

Insect Name: *Grasshopper*

Phylum: *Arthropoda*

Class: *Insecta*

Order: *Orthoptera*

Family: *Acrididae*

General Physical Characteristics: *Grasshoppers, like other jumping Orthoptera, have well-developed muscles in the hindlegs, giving them their exceptional jumping abilities. Unlike others of their order, they have short antennae. Their hearing organs are large and are located on the sides of the first abdominal segment. Most adult grasshoppers are winged, but some species are wingless. Adult grasshoppers vary in coloring and size, according to their species. Generally they range from 3/4 to 1 3/4 inches in body length. Most grasshoppers feed on plants.*

Typical Behavior: *Grasshoppers move from place to place by jumping, although many are strong fliers. Adult male grasshoppers make sounds to attract mates by rubbing together specialized frictional areas between the hindleg and forewing. Adult males also may make sounds to warn other males away, and both males and females may make sounds to warn other insects of the presence of predators.*

Habitat: *Grasshoppers occupy a variety of habitats, including grassy meadows, fields, and weedy places.*

Life Cycle: *The female grasshopper inserts egg masses in the soil and the young overwinter in the egg stage. Nymphs hatch from the eggs from late spring to late summer. They mature in about 60 days and undergo about five molts. Grasshoppers usually produce one generation per year.*

Materials

Computers and database or hypermedia software (optional)

As an alternative to completing the written portions of the activity sheet, if computers and appropriate database or hypermedia software are available, encourage the students to begin creating insect databases or hypermedia stacks or folders. Suggest that they create fields to contain the following information: insect name, phylum, class, order, family, typical adult body length, whether winged or wingless, coloring, food source, characteristic behavior, habitat, range of presence in the United States, mating habits, time of egg hatchings, location of eggs, period of growth to maturity, and number of generations per year. Encourage the students to build up their databases or add to their hypermedia stacks or folders as they read the poems and learn about their subjects. Tell them they will have an opportunity to demonstrate the use of their databases or hypermedia stacks or folders when the poetry unit has been completed. Finally, encourage them to use simple paint programs or the painting tools that are available in the hypermedia programs to illustrate their databases or hypermedia stacks or folders.

Materials

Paper; pens or pencils

Tape measures (one for each student group)

3. Jump Like a Grasshopper. Have the students estimate and record how *far* grasshoppers can jump in comparison to their body length (twice as far, three times as far, and so on). Have them estimate and record how *high* grasshoppers can jump in comparison to their body length. Challenge the students to verify their estimates based on research of reliable printed resources or on the basis of their actual observation of the insects. Then have them report their findings, indicating how accurate their estimates were.

Next have the students estimate how far they can jump in relation to their height. Tell them to set up and record ratios in which the numerator represents their height and the denominator the distance they estimate they can jump. Have them set up and record similar ratios of their height to the height they estimate they can jump. Then challenge the students to verify their estimates by actually jumping, recording their results, and matching them with their estimates.

Group the students in fours and have group members cooperate to measure and record jumping results for each member. First have each student jump forward from a standing start as far as she or he can. Other group members can make sure the jumper does not overstep the starting point, mark the spot of landing, and record the results. When each group member has jumped in this fashion, have the students set up new ratios according to their actual results.

Repeat this same process, having students do running long jumps. Repeat the process again, having students jump up as high as they can from a standing position. In this case you might first record how high they can reach while standing with both feet on the ground and then have them jump up from a standing position and touch a wall at the apex of their jump. Have students measure that height from the floor or ground and subtract from it the height to which the jumper was able to reach with both feet on the ground. Tell the jumpers to use the results in new ratios indicating how high they can jump in relation to their height.

Have the students compare with their original estimates the ratios they set up as a result of having jumped and measured. Finally, have them compare their verified ratios with what they have discovered about the jumping abilities of grasshoppers.

Extend this activity by grouping students in sixes. Have the first student in each group begin at a starting line you designate. Tell the student to jump forward from a standing start as far as he or she can. Then mark the spot at which the student lands and have the next student start from that spot and jump forward, and so on. When all six students in a group have completed their jumping, have them measure the total distance jumped. Encourage the students to try their jumping relay again, this time to better their total distance.

This jumping relay can be played indoors, on padded gymnastics mats, or outdoors, in a grassy area or on a running track. Running long jumps or jumping backwards may be substituted for standing long jumps.

4. The Grasshopper Chorus. Ask the students to describe what a grasshopper sounds like. Ask if they have ever heard many grasshoppers calling at one time and if so, to describe what they heard.

Explain the usual function of the grasshopper's sound: In most species

Materials

Instruments, objects of students' choosing to imitate grasshopper sounds the sounds, which actually are "calls" and often are called "songs," are made by males to attract females of their species. The female responds to the male's call by moving closer to the source of the sound. When the male and female are within inches of each other, the male may produce softer sounds to stimulate mating behavior on the part of the female. Once the two have mated, the male ceases calling until he is ready to mate again.

Explain that the sounds made by grasshoppers may be described as *mechanical*—they have no pitch. In other words, there is no matching musical note one can hum upon hearing a grasshopper.

Ask the students what they might use to imitate the sound of the grasshopper. (Perhaps two blocks of wood faced with pieces of sandpaper and rubbed against each other or a comb running across a fingernail.) Group students in fours and challenge each group to devise instruments with which they can create the sound of a rhythmic grasshopper chorus in which a number of grasshoppers "sing" together. Encourage groups to be imaginative. Suggest that they consider writing and performing songs in which the grasshopper chorus is incorporated. Invite each group to present its performance to the class.

Before the Reading

Prepare your students to read Paul Fleischman's poem "Water Striders" by using one or both of the following suggestions:

1. Ask the students if they have ever dreamed or imagined they could do something that is physically impossible (fly under their own power, run faster than the speed of sound, lift incredibly heavy weights, etc.). Invite them to share their imaginings with you. Share your own similar fantasies with them. Ask what there is about such imagining that makes it so delightful.

Tell the students that they are about to listen to a poem in which the insects the poet describes do something that appears astounding, even for insects. Encourage them to listen carefully to learn what the insects' special ability is.

2. Ask the students if they have ever attempted to teach someone a skill or operation easy for them to do but apparently difficult or impossible for the individual they have tried to teach. Ask: How did you feel when you were unsuccessful? How do you think the individual you were trying to teach felt?

Ask if they have ever attempted without success to learn from someone else a skill or operation the other person possessed or performed easily. Ask how they felt and how they imagine their teacher felt.

Share similar experiences of your own. Explore with students why it is easy for some individuals to learn particular skills and more difficult for others. Suggest that each of us has a variety of different abilities and combines those abilities in a unique way.

Tell the students they are about to listen to a poem that describes in a humorous way an experience of trying to teach a skill that is inborn to the teacher but apparently not possible for the student. Encourage them to listen carefully to "Water Striders."

During the Reading

Materials

Teacher copy of *Joyful Noise*

Tape recorder and prerecorded version of "Water Striders" (optional; a cassette tape, *Joyful Noise and I Am Phoenix, Poems for Two Voices,* by Paul Fleischman, performed by John Bedford Lloyd and Anne Twomey, available from Harper & Row)

Copy of *Joyful Noise* for student reader (optional)

1. Have the students listen as you play for them a reading of "Water Striders" that you and a colleague have recorded on audiotape in advance of the class. Alternatively, play the recording of the poem available on cassette tape from Harper & Row, publishers of *Joyful Noise.* Or, prior to class carefully prepare to read the poem aloud along with one of your students, you taking the left-hand part and the student the right-hand part.

Set the stage for your reading or tape playback by helping your students focus their attention on the poem. Ask them to imagine what it might feel like to be able to walk on water without fear of sinking.

Play the prerecorded version of the poem or read the poem to the students. Read with appropriate expression to help the students apply their imaginations to the poem. Emphasize the confident, matter-of-fact attitude of the water striders toward their singular ability and their sheer surprise that their students cannot follow in their footsteps.

Materials

Student copies of *Joyful Noise*

Tape recorder and prerecorded version of "Water Striders" (optional)

Materials

Student copies of *Joyful Noise*

Tape recorders for student use

Materials

Students' personal dictionaries

After the Reading

Materials

Writing paper; pens or pencils

2. Distribute copies of Joyful Noise to the students and have them follow in their copies as you play for them once again the prerecorded version of "Water Striders" or as you reread the poem together with the student with whom you practiced .

Ask the students what they pictured in their minds as they listened to "Water Striders." Ask if they were able to imagine the insects walking confidently across the surface of the water without sinking from view. If you previously asked your students to think of experiences of trying unsuccessfully to teach another a skill they themselves possessed, ask them now how the reaction of Paul Fleischman's water striders compares with their own reactions.

Ask the students what Paul Fleischman thinks of water striders. Ask whether his poem makes them think of water striders any differently than they may have previously.

3. Allow the students to read "Water Striders" again, silently. Then pair students and ask each pair to practice reading the poem, or selected portions of it, together. Have one reader take the left-hand part of the poem and the other the right-hand part. Tell both readers to read from top to bottom and to speak at the same time all lines printed on the same horizontal level.

Give pairs opportunities to record and play back their readings to help them achieve a smooth presentation of the poem. When they are ready, have them read the poem or selected portion to the class or to a small group within the class. Or they may play back a recording they have made of their reading.

Pair students who have difficulty with this form of oral presentation with more skilled students. Assist pairs as needed.

4. Have students add to their personal dictionaries any unfamiliar words they encounter in "Water Striders." Encourage them to seek from other students—reading partners, cooperative group members, and so on—suggestions about the meanings and pronunciations of the words. If you have distributed copies of the Glossary, encourage them to look up the meanings of the words and terms.

1. Poetry Idea: "If I Could...I Would" Ask the students to imagine they are able to walk on water, like the water strider. Ask how they would use their ability. Ask: Where would you walk? What bodies of water would you cross? What would be the advantages of walking on water? Would there be any disadvantages?

Invite the students to write poems of their own, inspired by Paul Fleischman's "Water Striders." Encourage them to write poems in which they imagine they are able to perform feats that now are physically impossible for them. Suggest they might begin the first line of their poems with the words "If I could...," and describe a feat they imagine themselves performing. Suggest they begin the next line with the words "I would...," and describe how they would use their imagined skill or ability. Tell them to alternate these two forms throughout their poems to give them unity and make them interesting to listen to.

Answer any questions the students may have about this poetry idea. Tell the students they might write serious poems in which they use extraordinary abilities to solve problems faced by humans or humorous poems in which they use incredible abilities to do nonsensical or fantastic things. If necessary, offer examples of the kinds of lines they might write ("If I could fly above the clouds/I would always find sunshine./If I could run like a cheetah/I would never be late." Ask students to suggest some sample lines and ideas of their own.

When you are confident the students understand the instructions, encourage them to begin writing. Circulate among them and offer assistance as needed.

Encourage the students to share with one another their work in progress. Have those who quickly complete their poems collaborate with students who are having difficulty or have them write an additional "If I could…I would" poem.

When the students have completed their poems, encourage them to read them aloud to the class. Respond enthusiastically, seeking clarification when necessary. Post the students' poems in the classroom. Save the poems you have posted, as possible contributions to a book of student poetry to be compiled when the poetry teaching unit has been completed.

2. What Do You Know About Water Striders? Ask how many students have ever seen a water strider. Ask those who have to describe what a water strider looks like, how it moves, what it eats, etc.

Point out that water striders are the most common insects that live on the water surface. Explain that they may be found in spring through fall at the edge of almost any still area of water.

Distribute to the students copies of Activity Sheet 1. Provide them with or guide them to resources they may use to gather information about water striders so they may complete the activity sheet. (See the Recommended Reading and Audiovisual Resources and Biological Supply Houses lists at the end of the literature teaching guide. Encyclopedias and books on general biology or the life sciences may also provide information to help students complete the activity sheet.)

In addition, if time of year and location are appropriate, encourage the students to gather as much information about water striders as they can simply by observing the insects in their natural habitats. Suggest that they make two-handled seines to collect specimens for observation. (See Activity Sheet 3.)

Tell the students that with care and quick reflexes they may be able to capture water striders in the seines and transfer them to clear glass, wide-mouthed jars so they can observe the insect closely. Tell them to punch holes in the jar lids and to put a little water in the jars along with some vegetation and perhaps some small insects. Remind them that they might also find a magnifying glass helpful in observing the details of the water strider's structure and coloring. Finally, tell your students to be sure to return the water striders to their natural habitat when their observations have been completed.

As an adjunct or alternative to observations individual students conduct of water striders in their natural habitats, arrange for students to conduct observations in the classroom setting. Have one or more students capture water striders, in the manner described, and bring them to the classroom. Or check to see whether live specimens are available from one of the bio-

Materials

Activity Sheet 1 (one per student, pair, or cooperative group)

Pens or pencils; drawing instruments

Printed resources about insects

Two-handled seines (optional; see Activity Sheet 3; one per student, pair, or cooperative group)

Clear glass, wide-mouthed jars (optional)

10-power magnifying glass (optional)

Rectangular aquariums, sand, water, green plants (optional)

logical supply houses listed at the end of this teaching guide. Place the water striders in rectangular aquariums with about an inch of clean sand at the bottom and two-thirds full of water. Add several green plants for food. Use stones to anchor the plants at the bottom. Cover the aquarium with fine mesh netting.

Encourage the students to observe and record the physical characteristics of the water striders, their eating habits, and so on. Encourage them to use the water striders as models for illustrations they make on their activity sheets.

Allow students to conduct their research and field observations individually, with partners, or in small groups of three or four students. Remind them that each member of a pair or cooperative group should be prepared to demonstrate the tasks each performed and that all students should be able to explain any of the information provided on the completed activity sheet.

When the students have completed their activity sheets, invite them to report to their classmates the information they have gathered. If information provided by students differs, have them cite their sources of information—printed materials, audiovisual resources, and field observations—and try to determine why there are differences among the reports. Finally, have the individual students, pairs, or cooperative groups keep the activity sheets they have prepared on water striders to combine in a class publication with similar activity sheets on the other insects featured in the poems of *Joyful Noise*.

FOR THE TEACHER

Insect Name: *Water strider*

Phylum: *Arthropoda*

Class: *Insecta*

Order: *Hemiptera (sub-order: Heteroptera)*

Family: *Gerridae*

General Physical Characteristics: *Water striders are slender, elongated insects with two sets of long legs, used to propel them, and one set of short legs, drawn up beneath the insect's head and used to capture and hold prey—small insects that fall into the water. Water striders appear to glide and skate over the surface of the water. They are able to do so because the tips of their legs are lined with tiny hairs that repel the water and because their claws are located well back from the tips so they do not break the water's surface tension. If the water strider's feet do get wet, it must crawl out of the water and onto vegetation until its feet dry so it can once again support itself on the water surface. The bodies of water striders are brownish-black in color. The insects may be winged or wingless and range in adult size from about 3/8 to 1 inch.*

Typical Behavior: *Water striders propel themselves across the surface of the water in a slow, gliding movement by rowing with their long middle legs, their long hind legs trailing. They make quick jumps forward—generally to capture prey—by using both their middle and hind legs. They detect their prey on the water's surface through use of sensory organs in their legs that pick up vibrations. Once the prey has been detected, they rush over to it, grab it with their two front legs, jab their beaks into it to stun it and dissolve its innards, and then suck the dissolved innards out.*

Habitat: *Water striders live on the surface of quiet waters or at the wet margins of ponds and streams. They hibernate among dry leaves near shore.*

Life Cycle: *During egg-laying time, from spring to early fall, the male water strider locates a fixed object in the water—a small piece of wood or plant —suitable for egg laying. It then attracts a receptive female by remaining at the spot located and giving off ripple patterns in the water by rapidly moving its middle legs up and down. A receptive female approaches the male, touches it with her leg or mouth and then holds onto the object the male has located while the male mounts her back for mating.*

The female lays eggs on the spot while the male stands guard. Nymphs hatch from the eggs in about two weeks. The nymphs undergo five molts, each taking about a week, before becoming adults. Water striders may produce as many as three broods per year.

Materials

Computers and database or hypermedia software (optional)

As an alternative to completing the written portions of the activity sheet, if computers and appropriate database or hypermedia software are available, encourage the students to continue building their insect databases or hypermedia stacks or folders. Have them enter into the fields they have created information about the water strider's name, phylum, class, order, family, typical adult body length, whether winged or wingless, coloring, food source, characteristic behavior, habitat, range of presence in the United States, mating habits, location of eggs, time of egg hatching, period of growth to maturity, and number of generations per year. Remind the students that they will have an opportunity to demonstrate the use of their databases or hypermedia stacks or folders when the poetry unit has been completed. Encourage them to use painting programs or tools to illustrate their databases or hypermedia stacks or folders.

Materials

Paper; pens or pencils

Dictionaries; thesauruses

3. Balderdash! Ask the students how Paul Fleischman's water striders react when told that their ability to walk on water is "surely a miracle." Ask if any students have ever heard or read the word "balderdash" before. Ask what it means.

Explain that the poem includes two synonyms for *balderdash: rubbish* and *nonsense.* Tell the students that the origin of *balderdash* is unknown. It is quite likely that someone invented the word because its very sound seemed to express to the inventor the notion he or she wanted to convey.

Tell the students that when a new word enters the language or when a word is given a new meaning, it is called a *neologism.* Tell them that slang often is full of neologisms in the form of new uses of old words. Ask the students if they can think of any neologisms in the slang they use. Once students have offered a number of examples of neologisms, group students in fours and give them ten minutes to respond to a two-fold challenge.

First have them spend five minutes brainstorming to develop and record as large a list as possible of neologisms, taken from slang expressions or other types or oral or written expression. In cases in which a word has been given a new meaning, have the students list both the previously accepted meaning of the word and its new meaning. In cases in which a word has been invented to convey a meaning, have them record the word and the meaning it conveys. Give the students access to dictionaries and thesauruses to assist them in their task.

Second, have the student groups spend five minutes creating and recording neologisms, that is, have them invent words to describe particular notions, situations, or feelings, much as *balderdash* must have been created to convey the notion of *sheer and utter nonsense*. Tell them they may use dictionaries and thesauruses to help them find words to combine into new words.

When the groups have completed their tasks, invite them first to report the neologisms they have discovered. Record them on the chalkboard as they are reported and ask students to judge whether the words suggested are indeed neologisms.

Then have the groups report their invented words and their spellings, without reporting their meanings. Have other students guess the meaning these new words are meant to convey. Then have the reporting groups verify or clarify the meanings of their neologisms. Have the class vote for the most humorous neologism, the most outrageous neologism, and so on. Encourage the students to experiment with the use of neologisms in poetry they write.

4. Surface Tension. Conduct the following experiments to help your students understand the phenomenon of surface tension, which allows water striders to walk on water.

Give each student a small paper cup, a medicine dropper, and a glass of water. Tell the students to pour as much water from the glass into the cup as they can without causing the water to overflow. Suggest they use the medicine dropper to add the last few drops of water. Then tell them to describe what they see. They will find that the water rises to a somewhat higher level than the rim of the cup and that the surface of the water has a skinlike appearance. Have them discuss what causes this phenomenon.

Explain that what they see is caused by the forces of cohesion between the molecules of water and that the phenomenon is called "surface tension." Because of the cohesive forces, the surface of the liquid tends to contract and to manifest properties resembling those of a thin skin, or elastic membrane, stretched over it.

Demonstrate the ability of water's surface tension to support weight. Pour some water into a wide-mouthed jar or similar container. Then have a student gently lay a needle on the water's surface (if the needle is slightly greasy, water will be prevented from creeping up its sides). The needle will seem to float on the water's surface, even though (if it is a steel needle) it is about seven times denser than water. Explain that the needle actually is being supported by the water's surface tension. Point out to the students how the water's skinlike surface bends under the weight of the object.

Repeat the demonstration using a paper clip or a double-edged razor blade. Have the students experiment with other lightweight objects to

Materials

Small paper cup, glass of water, and medicine dropper for each student

Wide-mouthed jar or similar container

Steel needle

Objects such as double-edged razor blade and paper clip; table fork

Variety of liquids (vinegar, milk, citrus juices)

determine whether the water's surface tension is sufficiently strong to support their object's weight. Suggest they might use a fork or paper clip to lower the objects gently onto the water's surface. If time allows, have the students experiment to learn of the surface tension of liquids other than water, for example, vinegar, milk, and citrus juices.

Finally, explain that water striders are especially equipped to take advantage of the surface tension of water. Their legs are fitted with sets of non-wetting hair, and their claws, unlike those of most insects, are set back from the ends of their legs so they do not break the water's surface. Consequently they are able to run on water with amazing speed and to stand on it with remarkable ease.

5. Pantomime. Pair students and invite each pair to pantomime the walking-on-water lesson a water strider might give another insect not similarly endowed. Have one student of each pair pantomime the water strider, walking confidently across the water. Have the other student pantomime another insect who watches the water strider and decides he or she also would like to walk across the water. Have the second student then pantomime requesting instructions and the two students pantomime the resulting lesson, with its inevitable consequences.

Give each pair an opportunity to present its pantomime for the class or for a small group of students. After each pair has completed its pantomime, ask the audience, "What did you see?" Congratulate each pair on its performance.

Before the Reading

Prepare your students to read Paul Fleischman's poem "Mayflies" by using one or both of the following suggestions:

1. Ask the students if they would change the way they are living if they knew they had only one day to live. Ask those who would change to indicate how they would do so and why. Ask those who would not to explain their choice. Ask students how knowing the length of time they had to live might affect the way they live.

Tell the students they will shortly listen to a poem about a creature whose adult life span lasts only about a day. Encourage them to listen closely as Paul Fleischman describes this brief moment and the activity that fills it.

2. Write the word _relative_ in large letters on the chalkboard. Ask the students for definitions of the word. Summarize the definitions on the chalkboard. If no one suggests it, explain that one meaning of _relative_ is "in comparison or relation to something else."

Offer some examples of this meaning of _relative_. For example, ask the tallest and shortest students in class to stand next to each and explain that relative to the shorter student, the taller student is indeed tall, but that relative to a professional basketball player, such as Kareem Abdul-Jabbar (7 ft 3 in.) or Shawn Bradley (7 ft 6 in.), the taller student is not so tall after all. Or ask the students to give the age of the oldest living members of their families. Choose a notably advanced age and explain that relative to that age, their own ages are young, whereas they are relatively old in comparison with newborns.

Tell the students they are about to listen to a poem that describes an insect whose life span, relative to theirs, is quite brief. Encourage them to listen carefully to "Mayflies."

During the Reading

Materials

Teacher copy of _Joyful Noise_

Tape recorder and prerecorded version of "Mayflies" (optional; a cassette tape, _Joyful Noise and I Am Phoenix, Poems for Two Voices_, by Paul Fleischman, performed by John Bedford Lloyd and Anne Twomey, available from Harper & Row)

Copy of _Joyful Noise_ for student reader (optional)

1. Have the students listen as you play for them a reading of "Mayflies" that you and a colleague have recorded on audiotape in advance of the class. Alternatively, play the recording of the poem available on cassette tape from Harper & Row, publishers of _Joyful Noise_. Or, prior to class carefully prepare to read the poem aloud along with one of your students, you taking the left-hand part and the student the right-hand part.

Set the stage for your reading or tape playback by helping your students focus their attention on the poem. Ask them to imagine what it must feel like to have to make every moment count, knowing full well when one's life will end.

Play the prerecorded version of the poem or read the poem to the students. Read with appropriate expression to help the students apply their imaginations to the poem. Emphasize the frenzied, fevered efforts of the mayflies to squeeze into a short period of time the activities of their entire adult lives.

Materials

Student copies of *Joyful Noise*

Tape recorder and prerecorded version of "Mayflies" (optional)

Materials

Student copies of *Joyful Noise*

Tape recorders for student use

Materials

Students' personal dictionaries

After the Reading

Materials

Writing paper; pens or pencils

2. Distribute copies of *Joyful Noise* to the students and have them follow in their copies as you play for them once again the prerecorded version of "Mayflies" or as you re-read the poem together with the student with whom you prepared the duet.

Ask the students what they pictured in their minds as they listened to "Mayflies." Ask if they were able to imagine the insects rushing about, trying to make the most of their "single sip of life." Ask how the poem made them feel and why.

3. Allow the students to read "Mayflies" again, silently. Then pair students and ask each pair to practice reading the poem, or selected portions of it, together. Have one reader take the left-hand part of the poem and the other the right-hand part. Tell both readers to read from top to bottom and to speak at the same time all lines printed on the same horizontal level.

Give pairs opportunities to record and play back their readings to help them achieve a smooth presentation of the poem. When they are ready, have them read the poem or selected portion to the class or to a small group within the class. Or they may play back a recording they have made of their reading

Pair students who have difficulty with this oral presentation with more skilled students. Assist pairs as needed.

4. Have students add to their personal dictionaries any unfamiliar words they encounter in "Mayflies." Encourage them to seek from other students—reading partners, cooperative group members, and so on—suggestions about the meanings and pronunciations of the words. If you have distributed copies of the Glossary, encourage them to look up the meanings of the words and terms.

1. Poetry Idea: "If I Had Only a Day to Live…" Ask the students to imagine they have only a single day in which to squeeze all they want to accomplish and experience in life. Ask: How would your life be different than it is now? What would you do? Where would you go? Whom would you see and talk to?

Invite the students to write poems of their own, inspired by Paul Fleischman's "Mayflies." Encourage them to write poems in which they imagine they have only a single day to live. Suggest they might begin the first line of their poems with the words "If I had only a day to live…," and use that line as a refrain throughout their poems. Suggest they begin the following lines with the words "I would…," and describe what they would do, where they would go, how they would act, whom they would talk to, and so on.

Answer any questions the students may have about this poetry idea. Tell them they might write poems in which they describe what they feel would be most important for them to do during their day of life or poems in which they describe fantastical things they imagine they might want to do. If necessary, offer examples of the kinds of lines they might write ("If I had only a day to live/I would have a going-away party with all my family and friends./If I had only a day to live/I would tell my family how important they are to me.") Ask students to suggest some sample lines and ideas of their own.

When you are sure the students understand the instructions, encourage them to begin writing. Circulate among them and offer assistance.

Encourage the students to share with one another their work in progress. Have those who quickly complete their poems collaborate with students who are having difficulty, or have them write an additional "If I had only a day to live…" poem.

When the students have completed their poems, invite them to read them aloud to the class. Respond enthusiastically and seek clarification when necessary. Post the students' poems in the classroom for all to read. Save the poems you have posted, as possible contributions to a book of student poetry to be compiled when the poetry teaching unit has been completed.

2. **What Do You Know About Mayflies?** Ask how many students have ever seen a mayfly. Ask those who have to describe what a mayfly looks like, how it moves, what it eats, etc.

Point out that mayflies are commonly seen in swarms above ponds or streams, most often in the month of May. Explain that each mayfly lives in its adult form for only a few hours or a day or two, although in their immature form, as naiads, they may live one to four years under water where few humans see them.

Distribute to the students copies of Activity Sheet 1. Provide them with or guide them to resources they may use to gather information about mayflies so they may complete the activity sheet. (See the Recommended Reading and Audiovisual Resources and Biological Supply Houses lists at the end of the literature teaching unit. Encyclopedias and books on general biology or the life sciences may also provide information to help students complete the activity sheet.)

In addition, if time of year and location are appropriate, encourage the students to gather as much information about mayflies as they can simply by observing the insects in their natural habitats. Tell them that with care and quick reflexes they may be able to capture mayflies in fine mesh sweeping nets (see Activity Sheet 2) and transfer them to clear glass, wide-mouthed jars with hole-punched lids so they can observe the insects closely. Emphasize that mayflies are delicate and short-lived, and that efforts to capture them for observation as live specimens may be less successful than efforts to capture and observe more robust insects. Remind the students that they might also find a magnifying glass helpful in observing the details of the mayfly's structure and coloring. Finally, tell your students to try to return the mayflies to their natural habitat when their observations have been completed.

Allow students to conduct their research and field observations individually, with partners, or in small groups of three or four students. Remind them that each member of a pair or cooperative group should be prepared to demonstrate the tasks each performed and that all students should be able to explain any of the information provided on the completed activity sheet.

When the students have completed their activity sheets, invite them to report to their classmates the information they have gathered. If information provided by students differs, have them cite their sources of information—printed materials, audiovisual resources, and field observations—and

Materials

Activity Sheet 1 (one per student, pair or cooperative group)

Printed resources about insects

Pens or pencils; drawing instruments

Sweeping nets (optional; see Activity Sheet 2)

Clear glass, wide-mouthed jars (optional)

10-power magnifying glass (optional)

try to determine why there are differences among the reports. Finally, have the individual students, pairs, or cooperative groups keep the activity sheets they have prepared on mayflies to combine in a class publication with similar activity sheets on the other insects featured in the poems of *Joyful Noise*.

For the Teacher

Insect Name: *Mayfly*

Phylum: *Arthropoda*

Class: *Insecta*

Order: *Ephemeroptera*

Family: *There are several families of mayflies, including Ephemerellidae and Heptageniidae.*

General Physical Characteristics: *Adult mayflies are small to medium-sized, slender-bodied insects that range in body length from 1/8 to 1 1/8 inches. They are brown or yellowish in color and their triangular wings, held over their backs, are glassy in appearance. Two or three long, hair-like tails extend from the end of the insect's abdomen. Adult mayflies lack functional mouthparts and thus do not feed. They live only a few hours or a day or two, although in their immature aquatic form they may live for one to four years.*

Typical Behavior: *Mayflies leave the water as pre-adult winged forms with poor flight abilities. After about a day, however, these forms molt to become glassy-winged, graceful flying adults. Mayflies are the only insects that molt in a winged state. They are commonly seen in swarms, flying in a dipping pattern above ponds and streams.*

Habitat: *Mayflies live near rivers, streams, and ponds and are found throughout North America.*

Life Cycle: *Mating and egg laying occur quickly over water, after which the adults die. The mayfly nymphs, or naiads, live under water, in mud, or under stones and logs from one to four years. Aquatic nymphs breathe by means of feathery gills located along the sides of their abdomens and feed on debris and small animals. In turn they represent a staple in the diet of many predators, including fish. The last-stage naiads molt into winged forms, leave the water, and soon molt again into the adult form.*

Materials

Computers and database or hypermedia software

As an alternative to completing the written portions of the activity sheet, if computers and appropriate database or hypermedia software are available, encourage the students to continue building their insect databases or hypermedia stacks or folders. Have them enter into the fields they have created information about the mayfly's name, phylum, class, order, family, typical adult body length, whether winged or wingless, coloring, food source, characteristic behavior, habitat, range of presence in the United States, mating habits, location of eggs, time of egg hatching, period of growth to maturity, and number of generations per year. Remind the students that they will have an opportunity to demonstrate the use of their databases and hypermedia stacks or folders when the poetry unit has been completed. Encourage them to use painting programs or tools to illustrate their databases or hypermedia stacks or folders.

3. Hurry! Hurry! Ask the students why the activity of the mayflies appears to be so hurried. Explore with them how the knowledge that we have only a little time available to complete a lot of work, or to have a lot of fun, often makes us hurry so we can get the job done or enjoy ourselves to the full.

Invite them to join in a game in which the object is to hurry. Divide the class members into two equal teams and have them take their places on opposite sides of a volleyball net. Explain that the game begins when one player throws the ball over the net to the other team. The player who catches the ball throws it back. The player who throws it back again must be one who has not yet done so, Thus, if a person who already has thrown the ball over the net catches it, he or she must pass it to a teammate who has not yet thrown it. Tell the students you will time them to find out how quickly both teams can make sure that everyone on each side has had an opportunity to throw the ball over the net. Ask the students to estimate how long it will take them to complete the game.

When the game has ended—when every player has thrown the ball over the net—reveal the elapsed time to the players. Challenge them to try again, this time to beat the clock. Continue as long as the students' interest remains high. Encourage them to invent variations on the game; for example, they might decide that the ball can be thrown only from a particular spot on the floor or playing field or that every player must have an opportunity not only to throw the ball but also to catch it.

4. Comparisons. Refer the students to the first six lines of Paul Fleischman's "Mayflies." Ask what the poet is doing with those lines (comparing the human life span with the life span of the adult mayfly). Point out that one of the most striking things about the way in which Fleischman draws his comparisons is his economy of words: In a mere 13 words he manages to make us aware of how relatively fleeting the mayfly's life span is.

Ask the students if Fleischman's comparison helps them appreciate better just how short a life span the mayfly has. Ask if they think it would have been more effective to draw a mathematical comparison, for example: The adult mayfly's life span is only about $1/25,550$ as long as that of the average human.

Ask the students for examples of other comparisons that use few words to make the similarities and differences between objects or notions clear and concrete. If necessary, offer examples of your own. (A comparison of a rich person and a beggar from the beggar's point of view, for example, might read: "Your millions/my pennies/Your mansion/my doorway/Your sumptuous feast/my table scraps.")

When you are confident students understand how to make comparisons concrete and striking by using only a few words, invite them, individually or in pairs, to follow Fleischman's example in drawing comparisons in as few words as possible. Tell them they may compare whatever they wish— objects in nature, attitudes, ways of living, and so on. Suggest some specific

Materials

Volleyball; volleyball net

Stopwatch

Materials

Paper; pens or pencils

items that might be compared, such as a race car and an economy car, a young person and an old person, a computer and a manual typewriter.

Circulate among the students and offer assistance as appropriate. When the students have completed their comparisons, invite them to share them with the class. Respond appreciatively and enthusiastically. Post the comparisons for all the students to read.

Before the Reading

Prepare your students to read Paul Fleischman's poem "Fireflies" by using one or both of the following suggestions:

1. Ask the students to name different ways of *signaling* without using words. Write their suggestions on the chalkboard. Suggestions may include use of hand or other bodily gestures, smoke signals, Morse code, and semaphores. Ask if any students have ever used any of these signaling systems and to demonstrate or explain them, if they can. Ask them in what situations we might prefer to use such signaling systems rather than simply express ourselves in words.

Tell the students they are about to listen to a poem about an insect whose ability to signal is what gives it its name. Encourage them to listen closely to discover what that insect is.

2. Ask how many students have ever attended a fireworks show on a dark night. Ask what they enjoyed about it. Ask if the show would have been less enjoyable had it been held during the day, and if so, why. Emphasize that the noise level probably would not have been any different but that the sometimes spectacular effects of light against a background of darkness would have been lost.

Tell the students they are about to listen to a poem describing an insect that provides an enjoyable light show of its own against the background of the night's darkness. Encourage them to listen carefully to discover what the insect is called and what it does.

During the Reading

Materials

Teacher copy of *Joyful Noise*

Tape recorder and prerecorded version of "Fireflies" (optional; a cassette tape, *Joyful Noise and I Am Phoenix, Poems for Two Voices,* by Paul Fleischman, performed by John Bedford Lloyd and Anne Twomey, available from Harper & Row)

Copy of *Joyful Noise* for student reader (optional)

Materials

Student copies of *Joyful Noise*

Tape recorder and prerecorded version of "Fireflies" (optional)

1. Have the students listen as you play for them a reading of "Fireflies" that you and a colleague have recorded on audiotape in advance of the class. Alternatively, play the recording of the poem available on cassette tape from Harper & Row, publishers of *Joyful Noise*. Or, prior to class, carefully prepare to read the poem to them along with one of your students, you taking the left-hand part and the student the right-hand part.

Set the stage for your reading or tape playback by helping your students focus their attention on the poem. Ask them to imagine a large field of small, blinking lights against the background of night's darkness.

Play the prerecorded version of the poem or read the poem to the students. Read with appropriate expression to help the students apply their imaginations to the poem. Help them to paint in their minds' eyes flickering dabs of light against a dark background.

2. Distribute copies of *Joyful Noise* to the students and have them follow in their copies as you play for them once again the prerecorded version of "Fireflies" or as you re-read the poem together with the student with whom you practiced.

Ask the students what they pictured in their minds as they listened to "Fireflies." Ask if they were able to imagine the fireflies flitting about, here and there, adding dabs of light to the dark night. Ask what mood the poem evokes in them.

Materials

Student copies of *Joyful Noise*

Tape recorders for use by student pairs

Materials

Students' personal dictionaries

After the Reading

Materials

Writing paper; pens or pencils

Materials

Activity Sheet 1 (one per student, pair, or cooperative group)

Printed resources about insects

Pens or pencils; drawing instruments

Sweeping nets (optional; see Activity Sheet 2)

Clear glass, wide-mouthed jars (optional)

10-power magnifying glass (optional)

3. Allow the students to read "Fireflies" again, silently. Then pair students and ask each pair to practice reading the poem, or selected portions of it, together. Have one reader take the left-hand part of the poem and the other the right-hand part, both speaking at the same time all lines printed on the same horizontal level.

Give pairs opportunities to record and play back their readings to help them achieve a smooth presentation of the poem. When they are ready, have them read the poem or selected portion to the class or to a small group within the class.

Pair students who have difficulty with this oral presentation with more skilled students. Assist pairs as needed.

4. Have students add to their personal dictionaries any unfamiliar words they encounter in "Fireflies." Encourage them to seek from other students—reading partners, cooperative group members, and so on—suggestions about the meanings and pronunciations of the words. If you have distributed copies of the Glossary, encourage them to look up the meanings of the words and terms.

1. Poetry Idea: "I Am the Magical Messenger…" Invite the students to write poems of their own, inspired by Paul Fleischman's "Fireflies." Encourage them to write poems in which they imagine they have the power to write messages in the sky for all to see, whether in daylight or at nighttime. Suggest they begin their poems with the line "I am the magical messenger…" and use that line as a refrain throughout their poems. Suggest they begin the following lines with the words "I send this message to…," and write to whom they would send a message and what the message would say.

Answer any questions the students may have about this poetry idea. Tell them they might write serious poems or humorous poems—or a combination of the two. If necessary, offer examples of the kinds of lines they might write ("I am the magical messenger/I send this message to my mom: Please bake cookies tonight." Or "I am the magical messenger/I send this message to the President: Please keep our nation at peace.")

When you are sure the students understand the instructions, encourage them to begin writing. Circulate among them and offer assistance.

Encourage the students to share with one another their work in progress. Have those who quickly complete their poems work together with students who are having difficulty, or have them write an additional "I am the magical messenger…" poem.

When the students have completed their poems, invite them to read them aloud to the class. Respond enthusiastically and seek clarification when necessary. Post the students' poems in the classroom for all to read. Save the poems you have posted, as possible contributions to a book of student poetry to be compiled when the poetry teaching unit has been completed.

2. What Do You Know About Fireflies? Ask how many students have ever seen a firefly. Ask those who have to describe the settings in which they have seen fireflies. Ask: What does a firefly look like? How does it move? When can fireflies generally be seen?

Point out that fireflies are commonly seen around dusk, over meadows and lawns and at the edges of woods and streams. Tell students that if they look carefully at firefly activity, they will witness quite a complex system of signaling.

Distribute to the students copies of Activity Sheet 1. Provide them with or guide them to resources they may use to gather information about fireflies so they may complete the activity sheet. (See the Recommended Reading and Audiovisual Resources and Biological Supply Houses lists at the end of the literature teaching guide. Encyclopedias and books on general biology or the life sciences may also provide information to help students complete the activity sheet.)

In addition, if time of year and location are appropriate, encourage the students to gather as much information about fireflies as they can simply by observing the insects in their natural habitats. Tell them that with care and quick reflexes they may be able to capture fireflies in fine mesh sweeping nets (see Activity Sheet 2) and transfer them to clear glass, wide-mouthed jars with hole-punched lids so they can observe the insects closely.

Remind the students that they might also find a magnifying glass helpful in observing the details of the firefly's structure and coloring. Finally, tell your students to be sure to return the fireflies to their natural habitat when their observations have been completed.

Allow students to conduct their research and field observations individually, with partners, or in small groups of three or four students. Remind them that each member of a pair or cooperative group should be prepared to demonstrate the tasks each performed and that all students should be able to explain any of the information provided on the completed activity sheet.

When the students have completed their activity sheets, invite them to report to their classmates the information they have gathered. If information provided by students differs, have them cite their sources of information—printed materials, audiovisual resources, and field observations—and try to determine why there are differences among the reports. Finally, have the individual students, pairs, or cooperative groups keep the activity sheets they have prepared on fireflies to combine in a class publication with similar activity sheets on the other insects featured in the poems of *Joyful Noise*.

FOR THE TEACHER

Insect Name: *Firefly*

Phylum: *Arthropoda*

Class: *Insecta*

Order: *Coleoptera*

Family: *Lampyridae*

General Physical Characteristics: *Adult male and female fireflies exhibit substantially different physical characteristics. The bodies of adult males are elongated and winged. Usually adult males have a pale light organ at the hind tip of the abdomen with which they make controlled flashes of light. The roof of the adult male's thorax, which overhangs the head, often is marked with red or yellow.*

Adult females are flightless and often resemble larvae. They are flattened, segmented, and luminesce with bright green light .

Fireflies range in body length from 1/4 to 1/2 inch.

Typical Behavior: *Most fireflies seen by humans are males. They may be seen especially on early summer evenings flying somewhat unsteadily though the air over meadows and lawns, signaling to females below in patterns particular to their species. Females who see the males blinking their lights respond from their perches on or near the ground. When the male sees the female's flash, he responds in turn, signaling and moving closer to her until he finds her and they mate.*

The patterns of light that fireflies use to signal vary according to species. The patterns may differ according to duration of signal, the interval between signals, the number of flashes that constitute a signal, the distance the male flies between signals, the color of the flashes, and whether the signal is composed of one flash or many. Some species may signal for only about half an hour; others may signal for several hours.

Fireflies are carnivorous; they feed on other insects as well as snails and other small ground animals.

Habitat: *Fireflies live in a variety of environments, according to their species. Generally they may be found in open woodlands, meadows, and gardens.*

Life Cycle: *Female fireflies lay their eggs on or just under the ground, a couple of days after mating. The eggs may require up to four weeks to hatch, after which the larvae begin feeding, preying on snails and other small animals. In fall the larvae burrow under ground where they hibernate until spring, when they emerge and begin feeding again. In early summer they make a small earthen cell in which they pupate. Pupation lasts about two and a half weeks. Then the adults emerge and begin the life cycle once again. Fireflies produce one generation per year.*

Materials

Computers and database or hypermedia software

As an alternative to completing the written portions of the activity sheet, if computers and appropriate database or hypermedia software are available, encourage the students to continue building their insect databases or hypermedia stacks or folders. Have them enter into the fields they have created information about the firefly's name, phylum, class, order, family, typical adult body length, whether winged or wingless, coloring, food source, characteristic behavior, habitat, range of presence in the United States, mating habits, location of eggs, time of egg hatching, period of growth to maturity, and number of generations per year. Remind the students that they will have an opportunity to demonstrate the use of their databases and hypermedia stacks or folders when the poetry unit has been completed. Encourage them to use painting programs or tools to illustrate their databases or hypermedia stacks or folders.

Materials

Student copies of *Joyful Noise*

Activity Sheet 4

3. Same Sound. Draw the students' attention to the lines of "Fireflies" that read

We're

fireflies

fireflies   flickering

flitting

flashing

fireflies

Ask a pair of students to read those lines aloud. Then ask all the students to examine them carefully and determine what is striking about them. Point out all the words that begin with the sound made by the letter *f*.

Explain to the students that one sign of a well-written poem or story is the use of words and word combinations that sound pleasing to the ear or that catch our attention and make us want to read further. Tell them the lines they just heard and read represent one example of just such a use of words. These lines repeat the same consonant sound at the beginning of a series of words in a way that pleases the ear, that makes the lines memorable. (If you wish, tell the students that this use of words is called *alliteration*. Be careful, however, not to obscure the wonder of poetry and other forms of writing with bewildering rhetorical terms.)

Distribute copies of Activity Sheet 4. Tell the students to page through their copies of the poems they have read in *Joyful Noise* and to find and write down, on the lines provided on the activity sheet, as many other examples as they can find of this same ear-pleasing use of words. Tell them to look for instances of two or more words that follow each other or are near each other that begin with the same sounds. Have the students complete this activity individually, with partners, or in small groups.

Other examples of alliteration in the previous three poems include the following: "Grasshoppers/hopping/high" (from "Grasshoppers"); "Whenever we're asked / if we walk upon water/we answer..." (from "Water Striders"); "Your moment/Mayfly month"; "rising from the river..."; "this single sip of living..."; "We're mayflies/by the millions/fevered/frenzied..."; "We're mayflies/swarming, swerving"; "our final, frantic act" (from "Mayflies)."

When students have had sufficient time to complete the activity, invite them to share with their classmates what they have written. Have class members judge whether what each student has copied from the poems represents the kind of ear-pleasing sounds you have been discussing. Ask them what they think of Paul Fleischman's use of these sounds. Tell them that a good writer knows when to use such sounds and when their use is carried too far.

Invite the students to work individually, with partners, or in small groups to compose their own ear-pleasing phrases and sentences by using the same sounds in series of words. If necessary, provide some examples of this device. ("Slowly, silently, the stream wound through the woods." "...bulky briefcase..." "...cool, clear, cloudless morning...") Have the students write their phrases and sentences on the lines provided on the activity sheet.

When the students have completed this activity, invite them to share with their classmates what they have written. Solicit the students' opinions about their classmates' examples.

4. Secret Messages. Discuss with students that different species of firefly use different signal systems to communicate with members of their own species. Some species use longer signals than others. Some use longer intervals between signals. Some use different colors of signals than others, and so on.

Ask what means humans have developed to communicate only with selected members within their own species. If no student suggests it, mention secret codes. Elicit from the students different secret codes about which they are aware or codes they might have used themselves, perhaps when they were younger.

Tell them you will show them a way to write secret messages that only those who have the key to unlocking them will be able to read. Dip a toothpick into a small jar containing whole milk and use it as a pen to write a message on a piece of paper. Allow the students to see you writing but do not permit them to watch closely enough to see the words you are forming on the page. You might write words such as "We are all poets" or "Poetry makes us look twice."

When you have completed your message and the milk is dry on the page, hold it up and ask if anyone can read it. Then tell the students you will show them how to decode the message. Have them gather round as you hold the paper close to a burning, incandescent light bulb. Your message will appear on the sheet of paper, as the paper absorbs heat from the light bulb.

Ask the students to explain what has happened. Explain that as the milk dries, the residue blends with the white paper and becomes invisible. When heat is applied, a chemical reaction takes place in the residue that turns it dark, making it visible against the white paper. Tell the students that lemon juice also serves as a kind of invisible ink, useful for writing secret messages.

Give the students opportunities to write messages of their own and to exchange them with partners. Provide each with a small jar of whole milk or lemon juice, a toothpick, white paper, and access to a lamp with an incandescent light bulb. Students who have difficulty thinking of a message to write might be encouraged to write portions of their "I Am the Magical Messenger" poems.

5. Take a Message. Point out that fireflies depend on their singular method of communication to continue their species. If male and female fireflies were not able to communicate their messages to each other, their species would die out.

Ask the students to name instances when it is extremely important for humans to communicate accurately and efficiently. *(When surgeons and their colleagues in an operating room tell each other what needs to be done next during an operation; when a football coach sends players instructions for a particular play in the closing minutes of a close game; when a teacher gives directions for a final exam)* Ask them what it takes to be an efficient, accurate communicator, or messenger. Ask whether they think they qualify as good messengers.

Materials

Small jar of whole milk or lemon juice, toothpick, and white paper for each student

Lamp with an incandescent light bulb

Materials

A brief message written on a piece of paper

Tell the students that you will give them an opportunity to demonstrate that they are efficient, accurate messengers. Line half the students up on a playing field, about 3 yards apart from each other, and the other half on the same field, spaced in the same way, about 30 yards away. Have the two groups of students face each other. Select one player, take him or her apart, out earshot of the other students, and read to the student a message that he or she is to deliver. You might, for example, use words based on the poem "Fireflies" such as: "The flickering, flashing, flitting fireflies practiced their penmanship by adding dabs of light to the dark June night." Then have the student return to take the first place in his or her line.

Tell the students you have given the student selected a secret message to be delivered only to the first student in the facing line. Tell them that student must then deliver the same message to the first student in the opposite line, and so on. Tell them you will time them to see how long it takes for the message to get delivered to the last student.

At your signal, have the student to whom you have given the message run as fast as possible across the field and deliver the secret message by whispering it to the first student in the facing line. Tell the messenger to sit down on that side of the field and have the next student race across the field and deliver the message to the next student in the facing line, and so on.

When the last messenger has the message, have him or her race to the opposite end and announce the message for all to hear. Compare it with the original message you read to the first messenger. Tell the students how long it took them to complete the message delivery and ask them to account for any discrepancies between the message the last player announced and the message you read to the first player.

Repeat the process with a new message, challenging students to increase their speed and, if necessary, their accuracy. Repeat the activity so long as students' interest and energy remains high.

BOOK LICE

Before the Reading

Prepare your students to read Paul Fleischman's poem "Book Lice" by using one or both of the following suggestions:

1. List ten vegetables on the chalkboard and have students indicate, by show of hands, whether they like to eat the vegetables. Next, list ten musical selections, from both popular and classical repertoires, and have students indicate whether they enjoy listening to the selections. Finally, show pictures you have clipped from newspaper or magazine advertisements of ten different clothing outfits, five appropriate for females and five for males. Have male and female students in the class indicate whether they would like to wear the outfits intended for them.

Point out that some individuals prefer particular vegetables over others, that some are inclined to listen to particular kinds of music but not to other kinds, and so on. Ask the students how they account for those differences. Discuss with them the matter of *taste*, in the sense of personal preferences or inclinations. Suggest that in many matters, such as food, music, and clothing, differences are a matter of taste rather than a matter of right or wrong, better or worse. Ask the students to suggest other areas in which what one does or prefers is largely a matter of individual taste.

Tell the students they will shortly listen to and read a poem in which differences of taste are described in an amusing way. Encourage them to listen carefully to find out what the differences are and who demonstrates them.

2. Write the saying "Opposites attract" on the chalkboard. Ask the students what they think the saying means. Ask them to give examples that substantiate their belief either that the saying is true or that it is not true.

Encourage them to listen carefully to the poem "Book Lice" to see if it bolsters or contradicts their opinions regarding the saying.

During the Reading

Materials

Teacher copy of *Joyful Noise*

Tape recorder and prerecorded version of "Book Lice" (optional; a cassette tape, *Joyful Noise and I Am Phoenix, Poems for Two Voices,* by Paul Fleischman, performed by John Bedford Lloyd and Anne Twomey, available from Harper & Row)

Copy of *Joyful Noise* for student reader (optional)

Copies of works by authors mentioned in the poem "Book Lice" (optional)

1. Before presenting the poem "Book Lice" to the students, tell them some authors with whom they may not be familiar are named in the poem. List the names on the chalkboard (Schiller, Scott, Agatha Christie, Conan Doyle, Roget, Shakespeare, Mickey Spillane) and briefly describe their writing, referring as needed to information provided in the Glossary. If you can find copies of representative works by such authors as Sir Walter Scott, Agatha Christie, Sir Arthur Conan Doyle, and William Shakespeare, as well as *Roget's Thesaurus,* display them as you describe the authors' works. Emphasize the different types of writing in which the authors engaged.

Have the students listen as you play for them a reading of "Book Lice" that you and a colleague have recorded on audiotape in advance of the class. Alternatively, play the recording of the poem available on cassette tape from Harper & Row, publishers of *Joyful Noise.* Or, prior to class, carefully prepare to read the poem to them along with one of your students, you taking the left-hand part and the student the right-hand part.

Set the stage for your reading or tape playback by helping your students focus their attention on the poem. Ask them to imagine how they would feel if they were turned loose in a library filled with the books of their favorite authors, in a store filled with all their favorite foods, or in a shop filled with all of their favorite clothes.

Play the prerecorded version of the poem or read the poem to the students. Read with appropriate expression to help the students apply their imaginations to the poem. Help them appreciate how very different, yet very compatible, the insect characters in the poem are.

2. Distribute copies of *Joyful Noise* to the students and have them follow in their copies as you play for them once again the prerecorded version of "Book Lice" or as you re-read the poem together with the student with whom you practiced.

Ask the students what they pictured in their minds as they listened to "Book Lice." Ask if they were able to imagine the book lice slowly, enjoyably eating their ways through all their favorite books.

3. Allow the students to read "Book Lice" again, silently. Then pair students and ask each pair to practice reading the poem, or selected portions of it, together. Have one reader take the left-hand part of the poem and the other the right-hand part. Tell both readers to read from top to bottom, speaking at the same time all lines printed on the same horizontal level.

Give pairs opportunities to record and play back their readings to help them achieve a smooth presentation of the poem. When they are ready, have them read the poem or selected portion to the class or to a small group within the class. Or they may play back a recording they have made of their reading.

Pair students who have difficulty with this oral presentation with more skilled students. Assist pairs as needed.

4. Have students add to their personal dictionaries any unfamiliar words they encounter in "Book Lice." Encourage them to seek from their classmates—reading partners, cooperative group members, and so on—suggestions regarding the meanings and pronunciations of the words. If you have distributed copies of the Glossary, encourage the students to look up the meanings of the words and terms.

1. Poetry Idea: "Opposites" Begin listing on the chalkboard a number of opposites: tall/short, heavy/light, noisy/quiet, fast/slow. Ask the students to add to the list other appropriate pairs. Ask what the items listed have in common.

Invite the students to write poems in which they describe opposites. Suggest they might begin the first line of their poems with words such as "I am…" or " She is…" and the second line with words such as "But you are…" or "But he is…" and so on. Or suggest they might select two animals, two cars, or two pieces of music that are altogether different from each other and describe their opposing characteristics in alternating lines. Encourage them to tie their lines together at the end of their poems with a conclusion, the way Paul Fleischman did in his poem "Book Lice," in which the two lice acknowledge that they are attracted to each other despite their differences. Answer any questions the students may have about this poetry idea. If necessary, offer examples of the kinds of lines they might write ("I am quiet and shy/But you are outgoing./I am serious/But you are carefree/ I avoid large groups/But you thrive on them." Or "An elephant is enormous/But a mouse is tiny/An elephant lumbers slowly/But a mouse scurries quickly about." Elicit similar examples from the students.

Materials

Student copies of *Joyful Noise*

Tape recorder and prerecorded version of "Book Lice" (optional)

Materials

Student copies of *Joyful Noise*

Tape recorders for use by student pairs

Materials

Students' personal dictionaries

After the Reading

Materials

Writing paper; pens or pencils

When you are sure the students understand the instructions, encourage them to begin writing. If you have discussed the use of ear-pleasing series of words with the students, suggest that they try to include such words in their poems. Circulate among them and offer assistance.

Encourage the students to share with one another their work in progress. Have those who quickly complete their poems collaborate with students who are having difficulty, or have them write an additional "Opposites" poem.

When the students have completed their poems, invite them to read them aloud to the class. Respond enthusiastically and seek clarification when necessary. Post the students' poems in the classroom for all to read. Save the poems you have posted, as possible contributions to a book of student poetry to be compiled when the poetry teaching unit has been completed.

2. What Do You Know About Book Lice? Ask how many students have ever seen a book louse. (Probably few have.) Ask if any students have ever seen evidence of book lice. Ask those who have to describe what they have seen.

Point out that book lice are tiny, and thus difficult to detect, and that they are commonly found in homes and buildings that house cereal products or have wallpaper or books bound with glue.

Distribute to the students copies of Activity Sheet 1. Provide them with or guide them to resources they may use to gather information about book lice so they may complete the activity sheet. (See the Recommended Reading list at the end of the literature teaching guide. Encyclopedias and books on general biology or the life sciences may also provide information to help students complete the activity sheet.)

Since book lice are difficult to detect directly, it is unlikely that students will be able to observe them firsthand. You might, however, ask local librarians if they can supply you with any books that show evidence of book lice at work. Or you might encourage your students to seek such examples from librarians.

Allow students to conduct their research individually, with partners, or in small groups of three or four students. Remind them that each member of a pair or cooperative group should be prepared to demonstrate the tasks each performed and that all students should be able to explain any of the information provided on the completed activity sheet.

When the students have completed their activity sheets, invite them to report to their classmates the information they have gathered. If information provided by students differs, have them cite their sources of information—printed materials and observations of the work of book lice—and try to determine why there are differences among the reports. Finally, have the individual students, pairs, or cooperative groups keep the activity sheets they have prepared on book lice to combine in a class publication with similar activity sheets on the other insects featured in the poems of *Joyful Noise*.

Materials

Activity Sheet 1 (one per student, pair or cooperative group)

Printed resources about insects

Pens or pencils; drawing instruments

Books damaged by book lice (optional)

FOR THE TEACHER

Insect Name: *Book Louse*

Phylum: *Arthropoda*

Class: *Insecta*

Order: *Psocoptera*

Family: *There are about 12 families of Psocoptera in North America. The book louse is a cereal psocid. Its scientific name is Liposcelis divinatorius.*

General Physical Characteristics: *Adult book lice are small—measuring less than 1 mm (.0394 in.) in body length—and lack distinctive coloring. Thus, even though they are abundant in particular environments, they often go relatively undetected. They appear as minute brown specks moving over paper. Book lice are wingless, and have enlarged hind femurs.*

Typical Behavior: *Book lice feed on and may damage a variety of organic material, including cereal products, wallpaper, and bookbinding glue and pastes, especially if the material is slightly damp. It is not known whether their primary food is molds on such materials or the materials themselves. They also feed on dead insects.*

Habitat: *Book lice live primarily in urban areas, in homes and buildings that house cereal products or have wallpaper or books bound with glue or paste.*

Life Cycle: *The female of the species deposits her eggs on spots she frequents. Then she spins strands of silk over them to hold them in place. The eggs hatch in a few days, and the nymphs pass through six nymphal stages and become adults in three to four weeks. The entire life span of a book louse, from egg to death, is between 30 and 60 days. About half that time is spent in the adult stage. Breeding continues throughout the year.*

Materials

Computers and database or hypermedia software

Materials

Student-selected favorite books (one per student)

Class lists (one per student)

As an alternative to completing the written portions of the activity sheet, if computers and appropriate database or hypermedia software are available, encourage the students to continue building their insect databases or hypermedia stacks or folders. Remind the students that they will have an opportunity to demonstrate the use of their databases and hypermedia stacks or folders when the poetry unit has been completed.

3. Playing Favorites. Draw the students' attention to the favorite books of the two book lice in Paul Fleischman's poem. Ask the students to characterize the two lice on the basis of their likes, that is, to tell what kind of "personalities" they have based on their reading (eating?) interests.

Ask the students if they think they can tell what a person is like from what the person likes to read. Tell them you will give them an opportunity to discover whether their judgments are accurate. Invite each student to select and to bring to class the following day—from home or from the school, class, or public library— a copy of a favorite book or a book by a favorite author. Tell them they may select any type of book—fiction, biography, history, poetry, even a comic book—so long as it actually represents a favorite book or author. Caution them not to tell any classmate the title of the book they bring. Tell them to be prepared to share with their classmates

- their reasons for selecting their books, that is, what they like in particular about the books they select

- why they think the chosen authors are good writers

- the titles of other books the authors have written

The following day, have each student deposit his or her book in a large box or sack you provide in the classroom. Make certain that no other students see the books. When all the students have delivered their favorite books, take them out of the sack or box and display them where all the students can see and browse through them. Then distribute to each student a class list. Tell them to review the books once again and to match books with classmates by noting the book titles alongside the names of classmates they think brought the books.

When the students have completed their matching task, hold up each book in turn and ask for a few volunteers to indicate which classmates brought the books to class, and why they think so. When all the books have been matched with class members, hold up each book in turn once again and ask the student who brought it to identify himself or herself. Ask if any students correctly matched the book with the student. Then ask the student who brought the book to explain why he or she chose it, why he or she thinks the book's author is a good writer, and to identify other books by the same author.

When all the books have been correctly matched with the students who brought them, ask the students whether they learned anything about one another. Ask them whether they learned anything about authors or books.

If students respond positively to this activity, consider asking students to bring in favorite musical selections (tapes, CDs, even just the titles of musical pieces), pictures of favorite clothing outfits, and so on, and ask class members to try to match the items brought with the students who brought them. These activities may help students come to know each other, and perhaps themselves, better and will give students opportunities to make brief oral presentations about subjects with which they are familiar and comfortable.

THE MOTH'S SERENADE

Before the Reading

Prepare your students to read Paul Fleischman's poem "The Moth's Serenade" by using one or both of the following suggestions:

1. Write the word *irresistible* in large letters on the chalkboard. Ask the students what it means. Ask them to suggest objects or realities that some people might find irresistible, that is, appealing to an overwhelming degree.

Ask what they think might be the consequences of finding irresistible any of the objects or realities they suggested. Have them explain their responses.

Encourage the students to listen carefully to Paul Fleischman's poem "The Moth's Serenade" to learn what at least one member of the insect class finds irresistible. Ask them to try to determine whether the term *irresistible* means the same thing for the insect as it does for us humans.

2. Ask the students if they know what a *serenade* is. Explain that a serenade in general is vocal or instrumental evening music, meant to be performed out of doors. Ask for examples of this musical form. (Mozart's *Haffner Serenade* and *Eine Kleine Nachtmusik*, Scarlatti's *Serenade for the Prince of Stigliano*, and Roussel's *Serenade* are well-known examples.) If time permits, play selections from well-known serenades to acquaint students with the form.

Tell the students that the term *serenade* often has a quite specific meaning: a lover's musical performance for a sweetheart. In this case, it is a song sung by a man to win the affection of a woman. Ask for examples of this type of serenade. If time permits, play examples of this specific form of serenade. Ask students if such music would be effective in winning the heart of a lover.

Tell the students that they will listen to and read a poem Paul Fleischman calls a "serenade." Encourage them to listen carefully to find out who is trying to win whose affection.

Materials

Recorded examples of the serenade musical form for playback to the students (optional)

Playback equipment (optional)

During the Reading

1. Have the students listen as you play a reading of "The Moth's Serenade that you and a colleague have recorded on audiotape in advance. Alternatively, play the recording of the poem available on cassette tape from Harper & Row, publishers of *Joyful Noise*. Or, prior to class, carefully prepare to read the poem to them along with one of your students, you taking the left-hand part and the student the right-hand part.

Set the stage for your reading or tape playback by asking the students to imagine what it might feel like to be drawn irresistibly to something or someone.

Then play the prerecorded version of the poem or read the poem to the students. Read with appropriate expression to help the students apply their imaginations to the poem. Emphasize the moth's all-consuming desire to approach the light ever closer, to grasp it, to merge with it.

Materials

Teacher copy of *Joyful Noise*

Tape recorder and prerecorded version of "The Moth's Serenade" (optional; a cassette tape, *Joyful Noise and I Am Phoenix, Poems for Two Voices,* by Paul Fleischman, performed by John Bedford Lloyd and Anne Twomey, available from Harper & Row)

Copy of *Joyful Noise* for student reader (optional)

Materials

Student copies of *Joyful Noise*

Tape recorder and prerecorded version of "The Moth's Serenade" (optional)

Materials

Student copies of *Joyful Noise*

Tape recorders for use by student pairs

Materials

Students' personal dictionaries

After the Reading

Materials

Writing paper; pens or pencils

2. Distribute copies of *Joyful Noise* to the students and have them follow in their copies as you play for them once again a prerecorded version of "The Moth's Serenade" or as you reread the poem together with the student with whom you practiced.

Ask the students what they pictured in their minds as they listened to the poem. Ask whether the poem makes them feel any more favorable to moths than they previously felt.

3. Allow the students to read "The Moth's Serenade" again, silently. Then pair students and ask each pair to practice reading the poem, or selected portions of it, together. Have one student take the left-hand part of the poem and the other the right-hand part. Have them read from top to bottom and speak their lines simultaneously when the lines are on the same horizontal level.

Give pairs opportunities to record and play back their readings to help them achieve a smooth presentation of the poem. Tell them that when they think they are ready, they may read the poem or a selected portion of it to the class or to a small group within the class. Or they may play back a recording they have made of their reading.

If some students have difficulty with this form of oral presentation, pair them with students more skilled at it than they. Assist pairs as needed.

4. Have students add to their personal dictionaries any unfamiliar words they encounter in "The Moth's Serenade." Encourage them to seek from their classmates suggestions about the meanings and pronunciations of the words. If you have distributed copies of the Glossary, encourage them to look up the meanings of the words and terms.

1. Poetry Idea: A Metaphor Poem. Remind the students of the comparison poems they wrote before they began reading Paul Fleischman's poems (see Introduction, Activity 3). Recall how they began by comparing common items with things different from them yet alike in at least one way (a pencil is like a rocket, a piece of chalk like a snowy day, and so on). Ask what words are used to make comparisons *(like* and *as)*. Ask whether they can find such a comparison in "The Moth's Serenade." ("I drink your light/like nectar.")

Next ask the students if they can find any other comparisons in Paul Fleischman's poem that do not involve the use of *like* or *as*. Ask, for example, to what the moth compares the porch light ("bright paradise," a "shining star"). Tell them that the comparisons they made in their poems are *direct comparisons;* the student-poets told their listeners and readers directly that one thing was *like* another. Explain that the comparisons Paul Fleischman makes without using *like* or *as* are *indirect comparisons;* Fleischman suggests or implies that one thing resembles another by using a word or term applicable to the first thing to describe or refer to a second thing that actually is unlike it but is somehow the same.

If you think it useful, explain to the students that a direct comparison is called a *simile*. Tell them that an indirect, or implied, comparison is called a *metaphor*. Take care, however, not to obscure these poetic devices by using rhetorical terms that may be confusing to the students.

Point out that "The Moth's Serenade" is a long comparison (an extended metaphor), even though the words *like* or *as* appear only in one specific instance. Ask to what the moth compares himself. (a lovesick knight) Ask to what the moth compares the porch light. (his beloved)

Encourage the students to write comparison poems of their own, in which they do not use the words *like* or *as*. Suggest that they think about something that is *like* something else ("My pencil is like a rocket") but pretend it actually *is* that other thing. ("My pencil is a rocket.")

Tell them they might write poems that enlarge upon one such comparison, as Paul Fleischman does in "The Moth's Serenade," or they might write poems in which they start a new comparison in every line or two. ("A good story is a door/that opens onto a whole new world/The grass is a green velvet carpet/that squishes between my toes")

When you are confident the students understand the instructions, encourage them to begin writing. Circulate among them and offer assistance, if needed.

Encourage the students to share with their classmates their work in progress. Have students who quickly complete their poems collaborate with students who are having difficulty or have them write an additional metaphor poem.

Invite the students to read their completed poems aloud to the class. Respond appreciatively, seeking clarification when necessary. Post the students' poems in the classroom. Save the poems you have posted, as possible contributions to a book of student poetry to be compiled when this poetry teaching unit has been completed.

Materials

Activity Sheet 1 (one per student, pair, or cooperative group)

Printed resources about insects

Pens or pencils; drawing instruments

Sweeping nets (optional; see Activity Sheet 2)

Clear glass, wide-mouthed jars (optional)

10-power magnifying glass (optional)

Terrariums created of clear glass, wide-mouthed jars furnished with dirt and plants (optional)

2. What Do You Know About Moths? Ask how many students have ever seen a moth. Ask those who have (surely, almost all of the students) if they can describe the moth's distinguishing features: its size, color, behavior, etc.

Ask if all moths are the same or if there is more than one kind. Point out that "moth" actually is a name given to a large number of families of double-winged insects and that there actually are thousands of different species of moths.

Distribute to the students copies of Activity Sheet 1. Provide them with or guide them to resources they may use to gather information about moths so they may complete the activity sheet. (See the Recommended Reading and Audiovisual Resources lists at the end of the literature teaching guide. Encyclopedias and books on general biology or the life sciences may also provide information to help students complete the activity sheet.)

In addition, if time of year and location are appropriate, encourage the students to gather as much information as they can about nocturnal moths that are attracted to light simply by observing the moths that circle their own porch lights and other outdoor lights (white lights are more likely to attract moths than yellow lights). Tell them that with care and quick reflexes they may be able to capture moths in sweeping nets (see Activity Sheet 2; students may find that a net with a somewhat longer handle than the three feet specified is a more effective tool). Tell them to transfer the moths to clear glass, wide-mouthed jars with hole-punched lids so they can observe the insects closely. Suggest they place twigs or weed stems in the jars to give the moths something to hold onto and remain still. Tell them they might also find a magnifying glass (a ten-power glass is sufficient) helpful in observing the details of the moth's structure and coloring. Finally, tell your students to be sure to return the moth to its natural habitat when their observations have been completed.

As an adjunct or alternative to observations individual students conduct of moths in their natural habitats, arrange for students to conduct observations in the classroom setting. Have one or more students capture moths, in the manner just described, and bring them to the classroom. Or check to see whether live specimens are available from one of the biological supply houses listed at the end of this teaching guide. Place the moths in terrariums created by adding soil and plants to large, wide-mouthed jars (with hole-punched lids) placed on their sides. Encourage the students to observe and record the physical characteristics of the moths, their eating habits, and so on. Encourage them to use the moths as models for illustrations they make on their activity sheets.

Tell students they may conduct their research and field or classroom observations individually, with partners, or in small groups of three or four students. Students who work with others may divide the tasks required to complete the activity sheet, but each pair or cooperative group should be prepared to demonstrate the tasks each member performed and all students should be able to explain any of the information provided on the completed activity sheet.

When the students have completed their activity sheets, invite them to report to their classmates the information they have gathered. When information provided by students differs, have them cite their sources of information—printed materials, audiovisual resources, and field observations—and try to determine why there are differences among the reports.

Have the individual students, pairs, or cooperative groups keep the activity sheets they have prepared on moths to combine in a class publication with similar activity sheets on the other insects featured in the poems of *Joyful Noise*.

FOR THE TEACHER

Insect Name: *Moth*

Phylum: *Arthropoda*

Class: *Insecta*

Order: *Lepidoptera*

Family: *There are a large number of families of moths. Among families of moths that are nocturnal and are attracted to light are the family Gelechiidae, the family Cossidae, and the family Pterophoridae.*

General Physical Characteristics: *The various species of moth manifest a remarkable variety of physical characteristics. In general, each moth has two pairs of wings. The moth's body, which generally is rather stout, and its wings and other appendages are covered with scales, sometimes brilliant in color and sometimes quite plain. Like other insects of their order, adult moths have reduced or atrophied mouthparts and take their nourishment through coiled tubes used for sucking up liquid food, especially nectar, which is a honeylike fluid found in flowers. They have large, compound eyes; long antennae, or feelers, with which they find their way around; and well-developed legs. When they land, they spread their wings out flat or fold them down over their bodies.*

Typical Behavior: *Most moths are nocturnal and not distinctively colored, although some fly in daytime and are brightly colored. Many species are attracted to light.*

Habitat: *Moths occupy a variety of habitats, depending largely on their feeding habits.*

Life Cycle: *Depending on the species, the female moth lays eggs on various herbaceous plants or twigs in the spring or early summer. All growth takes place in the larvae, commonly called caterpillars. The larvae have functioning mouthparts, made for chewing, and feed on a great variety of substances, but the adults feed on liquids, including nectar and other plant secretions, honeydew, or water. Most moth caterpillars molt five times before they are fully grown, although some may molt as many as ten times.*

Some moth caterpillars molt for the last time in a silk cradle or cocoon, which they spin around themselves and hang in a bush or tree. Others change into pupae under leaves on the surface of the ground or even underneath the surface of the ground. Some moth caterpillars hibernate, but most are ready to change, or metamorphose, into moths as soon as they are full grown. Pupae occur inside silken cocoons or under the protection of leaves or the ground. The pupa is a lifeless-looking brown and black case underneath the caterpillar's last skin. Inside the pupa the caterpillar's chewing mouth is replaced by a mouth that can suck liquids, wings are formed, muscles change from crawling muscles to those used for flying, and sex organs become fully developed. A moth may remain in its pupal stage from 10 days to several months, depending on its species. When it is ready, it either dissolves a hole in the head end of its cocoon with a fluid from its mouth and enters the outside world as a full-grown moth or wriggles its way out from under the leaves that covered it or the ground in which it was buried. Adult moths may be short- or long-lived, but no change in size or form occurs once they have reached the adult stage.

Materials

Computers and database or hypermedia software (optional)

As an alternative to completing the written portions of the activity sheet, if computers and appropriate database or hypermedia software are available, encourage the students to add to their insect databases or hypermedia stacks or folders. (A listing of appropriate database fields is provided in descriptions of this activity for use with poems that appear earlier in Fleischman's collection.)

To extend the students' moth watching, encourage them to create from clear glass, wide-mouthed jars, rearing enclosures for moth cocoons. Tell them to put about an inch of soil in the bottoms of the jars. Then have them find cocoons hanging from twigs and snip off enough of the branches from which they hang so they can be arranged in a hanging position in the jars. If they find cocoons covered by leaves, have them gently lift the leaves and place them on the soil in their jars. Tell them to sprinkle the soil periodically with water to keep their cocoons from drying out. Tell them to observe and record carefully the process by which the moth emerges from the cocoon.

Materials

Compass

Two bar magnets

Globe

3. The Compass Needle's North. Call the student's attention to the line in "The Moth's Serenade" in which the moth describes the porch light as "my compass needle's north." Ask the students what this description might mean.

Ask how many students have ever used a compass. Give students opportunities to hold one and to walk around the classroom with it while they examine it. Ask why the compass needle always points in the same direction, no matter which way they turn.

Explain that a compass works the way it does because the compass needle is magnetized and is responding to the force of the *earth's magnetic field*. Ask if students have seen a demonstration of magnetic force using a magnet and iron filings. If they have not, have one of the students dip a bar magnet into a pile of iron filings. Before the student pulls the magnet out, ask the other students to predict what will happen. Then have the student pull the magnet out. Observe that the filings cling to both ends of the magnet and the rest of the magnet remains bare. Explain that the magnet's force is greatest at the two ends and that these areas of greatest force are called *magnetic poles*. One of the poles is the North Pole (N) and the other is the South Pole (S).

Give another student two bar magnets and tell the class you will ask the student to bring the two N poles of the magnets together. Ask them to predict what will happen. Then have the student bring the two N poles together and describe what he or she feels and sees. Observe that the two magnets repel each other and that the magnetic forces of the magnets act between them even before they touch each other.

Repeat the process, having another student bring the N pole of one magnet together with the S pole of the other magnet. Observe that the two magnets now attract each other and that the force of attraction begins to act even before the magnets touch each other.

Ask the students to summarize what they have observed: Like poles of magnets repel each other, and unlike poles attract each other. (If students have listened to and read Paul Fleischman's poem "Book Lice," remind them of the saying that ends to poem: "…opposites /often are known/to attract.")

Explain the operation of a compass in this way: It is as if the earth had a huge bar magnet stuck in it, one end pointing to what is called the earth's *magnetic North Pole* and the other to the earth's *magnetic South Pole*. This huge magnet serves to line up the magnetized compass needle in the same north-south direction. The S pole of the compass needle points to the earth's magnetic North Pole and the N pole of the compass needle points to the earth's magnetic South Pole.

Ask if any students know why the earth has a magnetic field. Explain that many scientists now believe that the earth's magnetism may be related to the circulation of molten rock inside the earth's core.

Ask if any students know how the earth's magnetic North Pole is related to the earth's *geographic North Pole*. Using a globe, explain that the geographic North Pole is at the tip of the earth's axis, at latitude 90°. The magnetic North Pole, on the other hand is located in northern Canada (above the Boothia Peninsula), at latitude 73°3′. Moreover, the earth's magnetic field drifts westward irregularly, an average of about 1° every five years. Navigation charts must be changed periodically to account for the movement of the north magnetic pole.

Finally, ask students to suggest situations in which a compass would be helpful. Ask them for instances in which a compass might not have the desired effect of pointing to the earth's magnetic north. Ask again what Paul Fleischman's phrase "my compass needle's north!" might mean.

4. Circling Moth. Ask the students what happens when a moth approaches a light. Ask them to describe the movement of the moth. Tell them you will introduce them to a game in which they can demonstrate the circling movement of the moth that Paul Fleischman describes.

Group players in sixes. Have the players stand, kneel, or sit in a circle, about arm's length apart. Give each group a ball, which will serve as the circling moth. Tell the groups to begin passing the ball around from one player to the next, each player using two flat hands, palms up. Tell the players the object of the game is to get the "moth" circling as fast as possible, without actually grasping the ball.

When the players have mastered this form of the game, have them use one flat hand, palm up, instead of two to keep the moth circling.

Ask the students if they have ever seen more than one moth circling a light at the same time. Give each group an additional ball and tell them to try to keep both balls circling as rapidly as possible.

As an alternative, form triads within the groups of six and arrange the players so that no members of the same triad are positioned next to each other. Give each triad a ball and tell the players to begin passing it as rapidly as possible in the same way—each player using a flat, open hand, palm up—but only to other members of the triad and in such a way that it does not interfere with the movement of the other triad's "moth." This variation will require considerable cooperation on the part of all the players.

Materials

Two rubber balls of almost any size per group of six

WATER BOATMEN

Before the Reading

Prepare your students to read Paul Fleischman's poem "Water Boatmen" by using one or both of the following suggestions:

1. Ask the students to describe the most vigorous, sustained physical activity in which they have participated. List the activities on the chalkboard or have a student volunteer do so.

Ask students how they felt when they participated in the activities they have listed. Ask what motivated them to participate. Ask them to explain whether they would do the activity again.

Tell the students they soon will listen to and read a poem in which poet Paul Fleischman describes what he interprets as a vigorous, demanding activity by a member of the insect class. Encourage them to listen carefully to discover the kind of insect he describes and the sort of activity in which it participates.

2. Ask if any students have ever rowed a boat. Ask what happens if a rower does not pull the oars on each side of the boat in unison.

Ask if any students know what a racing shell is *(a long narrow racing boat propelled by oarsmen)*. Have students who have seen a racing shell in action describe what they saw. Ask: How many rowers were in the boats you saw? What factors make for a winning racing shell team?

Tell the students they are about to listen to a poem in which Paul Fleischman describes a particular insect as a six-man racing shell. Encourage them to listen carefully to determine whether his description is apt.

During the Reading

Materials

Teacher copy of *Joyful Noise*

Tape recorder and prerecorded version of "Water Boatmen" (optional; a cassette tape, *Joyful Noise and I Am Phoenix, Poems for Two Voices*, by Paul Fleischman, performed by John Bedford Lloyd and Anne Twomey, available from Harper & Row)

Copy of *Joyful Noise* for student reader (optional)

1. Have the students listen as you play for them a reading of "Water Boatmen" that you and a colleague have recorded on audiotape in advance of the class. Alternatively, play the recording of the poem available on cassette tape from Harper & Row, publishers of *Joyful Noise*. Or, prior to class, carefully prepare to read the poem to them along with one of your students, you taking the left-hand part and the student the right-hand part.

Set the stage for your reading or tape playback by helping your students focus their attention on the poem. Ask them to imagine what it feels like to engage in a demanding physical activity.

Then play the prerecorded version of the poem or read the poem to the students. Read with appropriate expression to help the students apply their imaginations to the poem. Emphasize the water boatmen's vigorous physical effort to reach their goal.

Materials

Student copies of *Joyful Noise*

Tape recorder and prerecorded version of "Water Boatmen" (optional)

Materials

Student copies of *Joyful Noise*

Tape recorders for use by student pairs

Materials

Students' personal dictionaries

After the Reading

Materials

Writing paper; pens or pencils

2. Distribute copies of *Joyful Noise* to the students and have them follow in their copies as you play for them once again the prerecorded version of "Water Boatmen" or as you reread the poem together with the student with whom you practiced.

Ask the students what they pictured in their minds as they listened to "Water Boatmen."

3. Allow the students to read "Water Boatmen" again, silently. Then pair students and ask each pair to practice reading the poem, or selected portions of it, together. Have one student take the left-hand part of the poem and the other the right-hand part. Have them read from top to bottom and speak their lines simultaneously when the lines are on the same horizontal level.

Give pairs opportunities to record and play back their readings to help them achieve a smooth presentation of the poem. Tell them that when they think they are ready, they may read the poem or a selected portion of it to the class or to a small group within the class. Or they may play back a recording they have made of their reading.

If some students have difficulty with this form of oral presentation, pair them with more skilled students. Assist pairs as needed.

4. Have students add to their personal dictionaries any unfamiliar words they encounter in "Water Boatmen." Encourage them to seek from their classmates suggestions about the meanings and pronunciations of the words. If you have distributed copies of the Glossary, encourage them to look up the meanings of the words and terms.

1. Poetry Idea: Animal Movement. Ask the students why Paul Fleischman repeats the word "stroke" so often in his poem "Water Boatmen." Suggest that, among other things, the repetition serves to impress upon us the type of physical activity in which the water boatmen appear to engage, as they move from the top of the water to which they have floated, down to the bottom, where they feed and rest. (The repetition also reinforces the image Fleischman conjures up of water boatmen as six-man racing shells, coxswain and all. The coxswain keeps the rowers working together at maximum efficiency and sets the rowing pace by repeatedly directing the rowers to "stroke.")

Ask the students to think of other words besides *walk, run, gallop,* and *fly* that describe the activities by which other animals move about. Write on the chalkboard the names of some animals and ask students to say words that describe the animals' movements, for example: Snakes...*slither*, elephants...*trudge*, antelope...*bound*, rabbits...*hop*, pigs...*waddle*, cows...*saunter*, horses...*clip-clop*, and so on.

Encourage the students to choose one animal and a single word that describes its movement and to write a poem about it, using the movement-describing word as a refrain, the way Paul Fleischman does in "Water Boatmen." If necessary, offer examples of the kinds of lines they might write. ("Slither/I am a snake/Slither/Cutting a zig-zag path/Across a hot, dusty trail./Slither/I am a snake/Slither/ Escaping the mid-day heat/Silently searching for shade.") Ask students to suggest some sample lines and ideas of their own.

When you are confident the students understand the instructions, encourage them to begin writing. Circulate among them and offer assistance, if needed.

Encourage the students to share with their classmates their work in progress. Have students who quickly complete their poems collaborate with students who are having difficulty or have them write an additional animal movement poem.

Invite the students to read their completed poems aloud to the class. Respond appreciatively, seeking clarification when necessary. Post the students' poems in the classroom. Save the posted poems, as possible contributions to a book of student poetry to be compiled when this poetry teaching unit has been completed.

2. What Do You Know About Water Boatmen? Ask how many students have ever seen a water boatman. Ask those who have if they can describe the water boatmen's distinguishing features: its size, color, behavior, etc.

Distribute to the students copies of Activity Sheet 1. Provide them with or guide them to resources they may use to gather information about water boatmen so they may complete the activity sheet. (See the Recommended Reading and Audiovisual Resources and Biological Supply Houses lists at the end of the literature teaching guide. Encyclopedias and books on general biology or the life sciences may also provide information to help students complete the activity sheet.)

In addition, if time of year and location are appropriate, encourage the students to gather as much information as they can about water boatmen simply by observing them in their natural habitat: generally ponds but sometimes in streams or in brackish pools along the seashore above the high tidemark. Suggest that they make two-handled seines to collect specimens for observation. (See Activity Sheet 3.)

Tell the students that with care and quick reflexes they may be able to capture water boatmen in the seines and transfer them to clear glass, wide-mouthed jars so they can observe the insect closely. Tell them to punch holes in the jar lids and to put a little water in the jars along with some vegetation and perhaps some small insects. Tell them they might also find a magnifying glass (a ten-power glass is sufficient) helpful in observing the details of the water boatman's structure and coloring. Finally, tell your students to be sure to return the water boatmen to their natural habitat when their observations have been completed.

As an adjunct or alternative to observations individual students conduct of water boatmen in their natural habitats, arrange for students to conduct observations in the classroom setting. Have one or more students capture water boatmen, in the manner just described, and bring them to the classroom. Or check to see whether live specimens are available from one of the biological supply houses listed at the end of this teaching guide. Place the water boatmen in rectangular aquariums with about an inch of clean sand at the bottom and two-thirds full of water. Add several green plants for food. Use stones to anchor the plants at the bottom. Cover the aquarium with fine mesh netting.

Encourage the students to observe and record the physical characteristics of the water boatmen, their eating habits, and so on. Encourage them to use the water boatmen as models for illustrations they make on their activity sheets.

Materials

Activity Sheet 1 (one per student, pair, or cooperative group)

Printed resources about insects

Pens or pencils; drawing instruments

Two-handled seines (optional; see Activity Sheet 3)

Clear glass, wide-mouthed jars (optional)

10-power magnifying glass (optional)

Rectangular aquariums, sand, water, green plants (optional)

Tell students they may conduct their research and field or classroom observations individually, with partners, or in small groups of three or four students. Students who work with others may divide the tasks required to complete the activity sheet, but each pair or cooperative group should be prepared to demonstrate the tasks each member performed and all students should be able to explain any of the information provided on the completed activity sheet.

When the students have completed their activity sheets, invite them to report to their classmates the information they have gathered. When information provided by students differs, have them cite their sources of information—printed materials, audiovisual resources, and observations— and try to determine why there are differences among the reports.

Have the individual students, pairs, or cooperative groups keep the activity sheets they have prepared on water boatmen to combine in a class publication with similar activity sheets on the other insects featured in the poems of *Joyful Noise*.

FOR THE TEACHER

Insect Name: *Water Boatman*

Phylum: *Arthropoda*

Class: *Insecta*

Order: *Hemiptera (Sub-order: Heteroptera)*

Family: *Corixidae*

General Physical Characteristics: *Corixids, or water boatmen, typically have triangular, flat heads and alternating light and dark bands or crosslines on the thorax. They appear to be mottled gray or gray and black in color.*

Each of the water boatman's three pair of legs is adapted for a special purpose. The short, flattened or scooped-shaped forelegs are used for gathering food (generally algae and other tiny aquatic organisms but sometimes larger animals, such as mosquito larvae); the mid-legs are used for clinging while feeding or resting; and the fringed hindlegs, which are long, flattened, and oarlike, are used to propel the water boatmen through the water.

Water boatmen range in size from somewhat less than 3 mm to about 13 mm (.12 in. to .52 in.)

Typical Behavior: *Unlike backswimmers, members of the same order which they resemble, water boatmen swim right side up. Usually they forage for food in the bottom ooze of their water habitat, though some species may come to the surface to feed on mosquito larvae. Water boatmen swim somewhat jerkily but rapidly; they spend much of their time clinging to submerged vegetation.*

Some species are attracted to light and fly to it at night in large numbers.

Habitat: *Water boatmen are commonly found in ponds. Some may be found in streams or in the brackish pools that are found at the seashore above the high tidemark. They are found both in saline waters and in fresh waters, though most prefer fresh water.*

Life Cycle: Water boatmen attach their eggs to submerged solid supports, such as stones, sticks, and shells. Some species lay their eggs on the bodies or appendages of crayfish. The life cycle from egg to adult requires about six weeks.

Materials

Computers and database or hypermedia software (optional)

Materials

Appropriate lengths of thick, sturdy rope, one for each activity group described

Gymnastics mats

Materials

A variety of musical selections with recognizable rhythms, including music in a medium-paced 4/4 tempo

Appropriate playback equipment

As an alternative to completing the written portions of the activity sheet, if computers and appropriate database or hypermedia software are available, encourage the students to add to their insect databases or hypermedia stacks or folders. (A listing of appropriate database fields is provided in descriptions of this activity for use with poems that appear earlier in Fleischman's collection.)

3. Teamwork. Recall with the students Paul Fleischman's description of a water boatman as a "six-man racing shell/rolled into one." Ask what they think he means by that description. *(He may refer to the fact that the water boatman's vigorous activity gives a sense of the kind of concerted physical exertion one might expect from a six-man racing shell. Or perhaps the insect's six legs in motion as it swims to the water's bottom conjure up for him the image of a six-man shell striving mightily together to reach its destination.)*

Tell the students you will give them opportunities to exert themselves physically, together with their classmates, in such a way that they achieve a common goal. Group the students in sixes. Have each group sit in a circle, knees bent, feet flat on a gymnastics mat. Place a thick rope, tied together tightly end to end, in a circle in front of their feet. Tell each group member to take hold of the rope. Then tell all the group members to try to pull each other up to a standing position by pulling on the rope at the same time and with similar degrees of exertion. Vary the activity by adding or subtracting group members.

Add further variety by arranging a rope in a straight line and having groups of students line up in a seated position at either end of it, each student grasping a portion of the rope, much as standing contestants in a tug-of-war game do. But instead of challenging one side to pull the other over a line, challenge both groups to pull strongly and evenly in such a way that members of both groups are pulled to standing positions.

4. I've Got Rhythm. Ask if any students have ever seen a racing shell with several rowers and a coxswain. Ask what the coxswain did and how it might have helped the rowers. Explain that part of the coxswain's responsibility is to establish a rowing rhythm that will help the rowers row most efficiently and keep the shell on a steady course. Point out that the coxswain accomplishes this task by calling out directions in a steady rhythm, much like the "Stroke!" "Stroke!" "Stroke!" of Paul Fleischman's poem.

Ask the students to define, describe, or demonstrate rhythm. Ask what sort of activities require a steady rhythm to be done efficiently or well.

Demonstrate rhythm in the following way. Ask the students to find their pulses in their wrists, necks, or chests. Then ask them to make a noise—

"thump"—to match the throbbing of their pulses. Point out that a healthy pulse will have a constant flow, a steady beat. Suggest that rhythm is the pulse of movement in music or in bodily activities such as rowing.

Next, play portions of musical selections from a variety of repertoires, classical and popular, and ask the students to clap or tap a steady beat with the music. Tell them that what is important is not how loudly they tap or clap but how well they experience the basic rhythm of the musical selections.

Then tell the students you will give them an opportunity to demonstrate rhythm in bodily movement, as rowers in racing shells must demonstrate rhythm to be successful. Have the students stand in the classroom where they have room to move. Play for the students a musical selection in a medium-paced 4/4 tempo, perhaps a lively march. Tell the students to move to the rhythm of the music in such a way that they touch a raised knee on one side of the body with a hand from the opposite side and then touch a raised knee on the other side of the body with the opposite hand, and so on.

Experiment with other rhythmic bodily movements; for example, have the students reach behind the back to touch with the hand on one side of the body the raised heel of the foot on the other side, or have them reach up with one arm while sticking the leg on the opposite side out, and so on.

Give the students an opportunity to create and demonstrate similar rhythmic movements to a variety of musical pieces you have selected or they have chosen.

THE DIGGER WASP

Before the Reading

Prepare your students to read Paul Fleischman's poem "The Digger Wasp" by using one or both of the following suggestions:

1. Write the following saying on the chalkboard: "Talk is cheap." Ask the students what the saying means. Ask them for examples of situations in which words alone are insufficient and deeds, or actions, are required.

Alternatively, write the following saying on the chalkboard: "By their deeds you shall know them." Ask the students what the saying means. Ask in what other ways than by deeds some individuals might prefer to be known. Ask for examples of situations in which deeds, rather than words alone, might be the best indications of individual character.

Tell the students they are about to listen to and read a poem in which deeds are all-important. Encourage them to listen carefully to determine what the deeds described tell about the doer.

2. Ask the students how we let others know we care for them. List their suggestions on the chalkboard. Ask whether they think it sufficient simply to *tell* those we care for that they are important to us, that we do care for them.

Alternatively, ask the students how we know other people care for us. Summarize their responses on the chalkboard. Ask the students to indicate which of the signs of caring listed are the most convincing.

Tell them that they will shortly listen to and read a poem in which Paul Fleischman describes how one member of the insect world demonstrates care for its offspring. Encourage them to listen carefully to find out what the insect does.

During the Reading

Materials

Teacher copy of *Joyful Noise*

Tape recorder and prerecorded version of "The Digger Wasp" (optional; a cassette tape, *Joyful Noise and I Am Phoenix, Poems for Two Voices*, by Paul Fleischman, performed by John Bedford Lloyd and Anne Twomey, available from Harper & Row)

Copy of *Joyful Noise* for student reader (optional)

1. Have the students listen as you play for them a reading of "The Digger Wasp" that you and a colleague have recorded on audiotape in advance of the class. Alternatively, play the recording of the poem available on cassette tape from Harper & Row, publishers of *Joyful Noise*. Or, prior to class, carefully prepare to read the poem to them along with one of your students, you taking the left-hand part and the student the right-hand part.

Set the stage for your reading or tape playback by helping your students focus their attention on the poem. Ask them to imagine how a caring parent must feel in trying to do all the things that are required to make sure his or her child is safe and well-provided for.

Play the prerecorded version of the poem or read the poem to the students. Read with appropriate expression to help them apply their imaginations to the poem. Help them identify with the force of love that Paul Fleischman imagines drives the digger wasp mother to make sure her children will get a good start in life, even though she knows she will never see her children.

Materials

Student copies of *Joyful Noise*

Tape recorder and prerecorded version of "The Digger Wasp" (optional)

Materials

Student copies of *Joyful Noise*

Tape recorders for use by student pairs

2. Distribute copies of *Joyful Noise* to the students and have them follow in their copies as you play for them once again the prerecorded version of "The Digger Wasp" or as you re-read the poem together with the student with whom you practiced.

Ask the students what they pictured in their minds as they listened to "The Digger Wasp." Ask what mood the poem evokes in them and why it does so.

3. Allow the students to read "The Digger Wasp" again, silently. Then pair students and ask each pair to practice reading the poem, or selected portions of it, together. Tell both readers to read from top to bottom, one taking the left-hand part, the other the right-hand part, and both speaking at the same time all lines printed on the same horizontal level.

Give pairs opportunities to record and play back their readings to help them achieve a smooth presentation of the poem. When they are ready, have them read the poem or selected portion to the class or to a small group within the class. Or they may play back a recording they have made of their reading.

Pair students who have difficulty with this oral presentation with more skilled students. Assist pairs as needed.

4. Have students add to their personal dictionaries any unfamiliar words they encounter in "The Digger Wasp." Encourage them to seek from other students—reading partners, cooperative group members, and so on—suggestions about the meanings and pronunciations of the words. If you have distributed copies of the Glossary, encourage them to look up the meanings of the words and terms.

After the Reading

Materials

Writing paper; pens or pencils

1. Poetry Idea: "Caring Means..." Write the word *caring* in large letters on the chalkboard. Ask the students to list the different ways in which the mother digger wasp showed that she cared for her children. *(She dug a burrow for them to protect them and keep them safe and snug. She worked hard to provide them with food to eat after they hatched.)* Ask how the mother believed her children would feel when they hatched and realized what she had done for them. *(She believed they would know she held a deep affection for them and cherished them.)*

Ask the students how they know other people care for them. List their responses on the chalkboard. Ask how they show they care for others. List those responses, too.

Encourage the students to write a poem in which they tell what caring means to them. Tell them they might write about ways other people show care for them or ways they show they care for others. Suggest that they begin each line or section describing caring with the words "Caring means...." Alternatively suggest they begin each line or section with the words "Someone who cares..."

Answer any questions the students may have about this poetry idea. If necessary, offer examples of the kinds of lines they might write. ("Caring means offering a helping hand/Caring means lending a listening ear." Or "Someone who cares/Always stands by you no matter what/Someone who cares/Lets you make a mistake and still likes you.") Solicit examples from the students.

When you are sure the students understand the instructions, encourage them to begin writing. Allow students to work with partners, if they wish. Circulate among them and offer assistance.

Encourage the students to share with one another their work in progress. Have those who complete their poems quickly work together with students who are having difficulty, or have them write an additional poem about caring.

When the students have completed their poems, invite them to read them aloud to the class. Respond enthusiastically and seek clarification when necessary. Post the students' poems in the classroom for all to read. Save the poems you have posted, as possible contributions to a book of student poetry to be compiled when the poetry teaching unit has been completed.

Materials

Activity Sheet 1 (one per student, pair or cooperative group)

Printed resources about insects

Pens or pencils; drawing instruments

2. What Do You Know About Digger Wasps? Ask how many students have ever seen a digger wasp. Ask those who have to describe the settings in which they have seen digger wasps. Ask: What does a digger wasp look like? How does it move? Is there anything unusual or distinctive about its behavior?

Point out that digger wasps are commonly seen around flowers.

Distribute to the students copies of Activity Sheet 1. Provide them with or guide them to resources they may use to gather information about digger wasps so they may complete the activity sheet. (See the Recommended Reading and Audiovisual Resources and Biological Supply Houses lists at the end of the literature teaching guide. Encyclopedias and books on general biology or the life sciences may also provide information to help students complete the activity sheet.)

Since it may be dangerous to approach digger wasps closely, do not recommend that students attempt to capture specimens for individual and class observation. Allow students to conduct their research of printed resources individually, with partners, or in small groups of three or four students. Remind them that each member of a pair or cooperative group should be prepared to demonstrate the tasks each performed and that all students should be able to explain any of the information provided on the completed activity sheet.

When the students have completed their activity sheets, invite them to report to their classmates the information they have gathered. If information provided by students differs, have them cite their sources of information and try to determine why there are differences among the reports. Finally, have the individual students, pairs, or cooperative groups keep the activity sheets they have prepared on digger wasps to combine in a class publication with similar activity sheets on the other insects featured in the poems of *Joyful Noise*.

FOR THE TEACHER

Insect Name: *Digger Wasp*

Phylum: *Arthropoda*

Class: *Insecta*

Order: *Hymenoptera*

Families: *Sphecidae*

General Physical Characteristics: *Although a great many species of these solitary wasps are small, within the family Sphecidae there is a great variety of size and form. Some are slender and thread-waisted; others are rather stout. Most are equipped with digging combs on their forelegs.*

The golden digger wasp displays the sort of behavior Paul Fleischman describes in his poem. This species is relatively large, about 15 to 27 mm (about 6/10 to 1 inch) in adult body length. Its thorax is gray; its abdomen bright reddish orange, covered with golden pile.

Typical Behavior: *The female golden digger wasp usually constructs a simple burrow in heavy soil. Next it attaches an egg to the roof or wall of the burrow. Then it provisions the nest it has created by stinging and paralyzing a katydid nymph and dragging it along the ground to the burrow, walking backwards the whole way.*

The paralysis, which the wasp has induced with a substance secreted with its sting, keeps the prey edible until the wasp larva hatches and begins feeding on it. It also assures that the prey will not move away from the legless wasp larva. Finally, because the paralyzed host does not give off the odor of a dead insect, it does not attract scavenger insects.

Habitat: *Digger wasps live in a variety of environments. Golden digger wasps, for example, often are found in arid regions.*

Life Cycle: *Eggs implanted by female wasps on burrow walls or roofs soon hatch into legless grubs which attach themselves to the paralyzed katydid and begin eating it. After consuming the katydid, the wasp spins a cocoon in its earthen burrow and generally overwinters in this stage. The following spring or summer, the larva pupates and the adult wasp chews its way out of the cocoon and digs its way to the surface.*

Materials

Computers and database or hypermedia software

As an alternative to completing the written portions of the activity sheet, if computers and appropriate database or hypermedia software are available, encourage the students to add to their insect databases or hypermedia stacks or folders. (A listing of appropriate database fields is provided in descriptions of this activity for use with poems that appear earlier in Fleischman's collection.)

Materials

Drawing paper and drawing instruments

Modeling clay

Found materials (small cardboard boxes, cardboard cylinders, milk cartons, styrofoam, etc.)

Glue, cellophane tape

Materials

Writing paper; pens or pencils

Jar or metal container that can be sealed

Shovel

3. Safe and Snug. Ask the students what the mother digger wasp thought most important about the home she provided for her children. Recall with them that she took great care to make sure the home provided her children with protection from the weather and was safe and snug.

Ask the students to describe the features of a house that would provide its human occupants with protection from harsh weather or from anything else that might pose a danger to them and that would make them feel comfortable, that is, "safe and snug." List their suggestions on the chalkboard.

Tell the students you will give them an opportunity to design a house that would provide both protection and comfort. Tell them they may work individually, with partners, or in small groups. Tell those who work with others that each individual must be able to explain all the elements of the overall design when the project has been completed and to indicate their contributions to the design.

Invite the students to work in a medium with which they are comfortable. Provide them with as many materials as you reasonably can: drawing paper and drawing instruments for those who choose to draw their designs; modeling clay or a variety of found materials (small cardboard boxes and cylinders, milk cartons of various sizes, styrofoam, buttons, wooden toothpicks, matchsticks, etc.) for those who choose to mold or build small-scale renderings of their houses; and so on. Encourage students to bring from home other materials they want to use. Assure the students that they need not model their houses on current designs; tell them the only criterion for their designs is that their houses provide protection and comfort.

If students are able, suggest they build or draw their models to scale and indicate the scale on their completed designs.

Give the students sufficient time to complete their designs. When they have done so, invite them to explain the features of their houses and to point out specifically how the houses would protect and provide comfort for their occupants. Invite other students to ask questions about the designs presented and to make suggestions regarding how they might be improved. If the designs or models have been done to scale, have other students check their accuracy by measuring them and calculating the sizes of structures which the designs or models represent. Post or place the house designs and models in the classroom so students may examine all of them more closely at their leisure.

4. Advice for the Future. Ask the students what the mother digger wasp's greatest concern was. *(that her children would have a good life)* Ask how she tried to assure that her children's future would be good. *(She provided them with a protective environment and with food.)*

Ask the students what they think are the most important things they could receive from their parents' generation to assure them of a good future. Accept all reasonable suggestions and summarize them on the chalkboard.

Then ask the students to consider what *they* might give to people who come after them to assure that they have a good life. Suggest that since it is not practical to leave specific items of food, as the mother digger wasp does, perhaps they might leave advice about how to live a good life.

Group the students in fours and encourage each group to agree on one or two pieces of advice for people who will come after them. If necessary, offer examples of the kind of advice they might consider. Tell them that all the advice offered by each group will be submitted to the vote of the class and that the items accepted as most important will be written down, placed in a time capsule, and buried on the school grounds, to be unearthed some years later and shared with students younger than they.

When you have allowed sufficient time for discussion, invite each group to report to the class the advice it recommends. Use the reports as an occasion for students to discuss what is most important in assuring a livable future for everyone.

When the class has agreed on the advice it would like to pass on, have volunteer students write down the advice, either on separate pieces of paper or on a combined list. Have the students write a brief explanation of what the advice represents and why they are offering it. Seal what they write in a jar or metal container, along with the explanation of its origin and purpose. Then lead the students to a spot on the school grounds, which you have prearranged. Have the students dig a hole of reasonable depth (if feasible, have each student take a turn) and bury the advice, to be unearthed in some later year—for example, by students in the school's first grade when they reach the grade level of your students.

5. Knots and Tangles. Ask the students what it must take on the part of the mother digger wasp to drag the paralyzed katydid caterpillar, which often outweighs it, all the way to the burrow it has dug for its children. Ask to what the wasp credits its ability to do so. *(perseverance)*

Ask the students to explain what they think perseverance is. Elicit from the students physical or mental activities that require perseverance on the part of human beings. List their suggestions on the chalkboard.

Tell the students you will teach them a game that requires perseverance on the part of its players. Divide the students into groups of 10 to 12. Tell the students to stand in a circle, shoulder to shoulder, facing each other. Then tell them to place their hands in the center and to the grasp firmly the hands of two people other than those standing next to them on either side. Now tell the group to work together to untie the knot they have created, without releasing handholds. Warn the players that it may take some perseverance to get the knot untangled.

CICADAS

Before the Reading

Materials

Recorded joyful choral music selections

Recorded versions of a musical selection rendered by chorus and by a single voice

Appropriate playback equipment

Prepare your students to read Paul Fleischman's poem "Cicadas" by using one or both of the following suggestions:

1. Ask the students if any of them have ever heard a large choir singing, perhaps in a church or at a musical performance. Ask: How many singers made up the choir? What type of music did the choir sing? How did their singing sound? How does choral music sound different from music sung by a single voice?

Play one or two joyful choral musical selections for the students. Ask the students how the music makes them feel. If possible, play versions of the same musical selection, one sung by a chorus, the other by an individual. Ask the students if the versions strike them differently or make them feel different, and if so, how.

Tell the students that they will shortly read a poem in which Paul Fleischman compares the noise made by particular insects to the joyful singing of a large choir. Encourage the students to listen carefully to find out what kind of insects the poet describes.

2. Ask the students if they have ever had the experience of enduring poor or harsh weather for a relatively long period only to find it end with a gloriously beautiful day. Perhaps they endured a period of gray, cold, rainy days or of sleet and snow, which was followed by a wonderfully sunny mild or warm day. Ask them how they felt and why they felt that way. Ask whether the day on which the weather changed made them want to sing, dance, run, and play, or otherwise express their feelings.

Tell the students they are about to listen to a poem in which a long period of darkness is followed by a period of sun, heat, and light. Encourage the students to listen carefully to determine the effect of this change as described by poet Paul Fleischman.

During the Reading

Materials

Teacher copy of *Joyful Noise*

Tape recorder and prerecorded version of "Cicadas" (optional; a cassette tape, *Joyful Noise and I Am Phoenix, Poems for Two Voices,* by Paul Fleischman, performed by John Bedford Lloyd and Anne Twomey, available from Harper & Row)

Copy of *Joyful Noise* for student reader (optional)

1. Have the students listen as you play for them a reading of "Cicadas" that you and a colleague have recorded on audiotape in advance of the class. Alternatively, play the recording of the poem available on cassette tape from Harper & Row, publishers of *Joyful Noise*. Or, prior to class, carefully prepare to read the poem to them along with one of your students, you taking the left-hand part and the student the right-hand part.

Set the stage for your reading or tape playback by helping your students focus their attention on the poem. Ask them to imagine themselves outdoors on a warm, sunny, mid-August day and to think about how they would feel and what they might hear.

Play the prerecorded version of the poem or read the poem to the students. Read with appropriate expression to help the students apply their imaginations to the poem.

Materials

Student copies of *Joyful Noise*

Tape recorder and prerecorded version of "Cicadas" (optional)

Materials

Student copies of *Joyful Noise*

Tape recorders for use by student pairs

Materials

Students' personal dictionaries

After the Reading

2. Distribute copies of *Joyful Noise* to the students and have them follow in their copies as you play for them once again the prerecorded version of "Cicadas" or as you re-read the poem together with the student with whom you practiced.

Ask the students what they pictured in their minds as they listened to "Cicadas." Ask what mood the poem evokes in them.

3. Allow the students to read "Cicadas" again, silently. Then pair students and ask each pair to practice reading the poem, or selected portions of it, together. Have one reader take the left-hand part of the poem and the other the right-hand part, both speaking at the same time all lines printed on the same horizontal level.

Give pairs opportunities to record and play back their readings to help them achieve a smooth presentation of the poem. When they are ready, have them read the poem or selected portion to the class or to a small group within the class. Or they may play back a recording they have made of their reading.

Pair students who have difficulty with this oral presentation with more skilled students. Assist pairs as needed.

4. Have students add to their personal dictionaries any unfamiliar words they encounter in "Cicadas." Encourage them to seek from other students—reading partners, cooperative group members, and so on—suggestions about the meanings and pronunciations of the words. If you have distributed copies of the Glossary, encourage them to look up the meanings of the words and terms.

1. Poetic Devices. Ask the students to reread "Cicadas" silently to themselves and to try to find some of the different ways of using words to please the ear and have an effect on listeners that the class has noted in other Paul Fleischman poems or perhaps in poems of their own. Summarize their findings on the chalkboard.

Observant students will note Fleischman's effective use of

- implied comparisons, or *metaphor:* "Air kiln-hot, lead heavy"; the extended comparison of the gathering of cicadas to the assembling of a mighty choir to sing joyful hymns of praise

- repetition of the same consonant sound at the beginning of series of words, or *alliteration:* "splitting skins/and singing"; "booming/ boisterous /joyful noise!"

- repeated use of the word ending *-ing,* perhaps to create a sense of the way cicadas actually sound or to create a sense of movement: "singing…humming…buzzing… assembling…droning…breaking ground…splitting skins; …singing…rejoicing…whining…whirring… pulsing…chanting…sending forth."

Encourage the students to try to use such poetic devices in their own poetry (see following).

Materials

Writing paper; pens or pencils

2. Poetry Idea: Joyful Noises. Ask the students to think about joyful noises they have heard. It may be the sound of the school bell marking the end of the school day, the sound of an ice cream truck coming down the street on a hot summer day, or the sound of an umpire yelling "Play ball!" It may be the voice of a loved one who has been away, a telephone ring announcing an expected call from a good friend, or a chorus of voices singing "Happy Birthday!" Summarize the students' suggestions on the chalkboard.

Invite the students to write poems of their own, inspired by Paul Fleischman's "Cicadas," about joyful noises they enjoy hearing. Suggest they begin their poems with the line "I love to hear…" and use that line as a refrain throughout their poems. Suggest that each line or couplet describe at least one joyful noise.

Answer any questions the students may have about this poetry idea. If necessary, offer examples of the kinds of lines they might write. ("I love to hear/my dog barking when I come home/I love to hear/a train whistling down the tracks.") Elicit other examples from the students.

When you are sure the students understand the instructions, encourage them to begin writing. Circulate among them and offer assistance.

Encourage the students to share with one another their work in progress. Have those who complete their poems quickly work together with students who are having difficulty, or have them write an additional joyful noise poem.

When the students have completed their poems, invite them to read them aloud to the class. Respond enthusiastically, seeking clarification when necessary. Post the students' poems in the classroom for all to read. Save the poems you have posted, as possible contributions to a book of student poetry to be compiled when the poetry teaching unit has been completed.

Materials

Activity Sheet 1 (one per student, pair, or cooperative group)

Printed resources about insects

Pens or pencils; drawing instruments

Sweeping nets (optional; see Activity Sheet 2)

Clear glass, wide-mouthed jars (optional)

10-power magnifying glass (optional)

3. What Do You Know About Cicadas? Ask how many students have ever seen or heard a cicada. Ask those who have to describe the settings in which they have seen or heard one. Ask: What does a cicada look like? How does it move? What does it sound like? When can cicadas generally be seen?

Point out that cicadas are commonly seen and heard in North America in summer and may be found in a variety of habitats ranging from forests and woodlands to deserts. They are typically found in tall shade trees.

Distribute to the students copies of Activity Sheet 1. Provide them with or guide them to resources they may use to gather information about cicadas so they may complete the activity sheet. (See the Recommended Reading and Audiovisual Resources and Biological Supply Houses lists at the end of the literature teaching guide. Encyclopedias and books on general biology or the life sciences may also provide information to help students complete the activity sheet.)

In addition, if time of year and location are appropriate, encourage the students to gather as much information about cicadas as they can simply by observing the insects in their natural habitats. Tell them that with luck, care, and quick reflexes they may be able to capture cicadas in fine mesh sweeping nets (see Activity Sheet 2) and transfer them to clear glass, wide-mouthed jars with hole-punched lids so they can observe the insects closely.

Remind the students that they might also find a magnifying glass helpful in observing the details of the cicada's structure and coloring. Finally, tell your students to be sure to return the cicadas to their natural habitat when their observations have been completed.

As an adjunct or alternative to observations individual students conduct of cicadas in their natural habitats, arrange for students to conduct observations in the classroom setting. Have one or more students capture cicadas, in the manner just described, and bring them to the classroom. Or check to see whether live specimens are available from the biological supply houses listed at the end of this teaching guide. Place the cicadas in terrariums created by adding soil and plants to large, wide-mouthed jars placed on their sides. (Tell students to make sure the jar lids have air holes punched in them.) Encourage the students to observe and record the physical characteristics of the cicadas, their eating habits, and so on. Encourage them to use the cicadas as models for illustrations they make on their activity sheets.

Allow students to conduct their research and field observations individually, with partners, or in small groups of three or four students. Remind them that each member of a pair or cooperative group should be prepared to demonstrate the tasks each performed and that all students should be able to explain any of the information provided on the completed activity sheet.

When the students have completed their activity sheets, invite them to report to their classmates the information they have gathered. If information provided by students differs, have them cite their sources of information—printed materials, audiovisual resources, and field observations—and try to determine why there are differences among the reports. Finally, have the individual students, pairs, or cooperative groups keep the activity sheets they have prepared on cicadas to combine in a class publication with similar activity sheets on the other insects featured in the poems of *Joyful Noise*.

FOR THE TEACHER

Insect Name: *Cicada*

Phylum: *Arthropoda*

Class: *Insecta*

Order: *Hemiptera*

Suborder: *Homoptera*

Family: *Cicadidae*

General Physical Characteristics: *Adult cicadas of most species are medium to large in size, ranging from 1 to 2 1/2 inches in body length. They have wide, blunt heads with bulging eyes; large, clear, membranous wings that may be tinted green, yellow, or orange; and sturdy legs.*

Cicada nymphs, which remain underground during their lengthy developmental period, have front legs that are enlarged for digging. The nymphs feed on the sap of roots of deciduous trees; adults suck juices from the limbs and twigs of trees.

Typical Behavior: *Cicadas are most noted for the buzzing, whining, droning sound produced in most species by the males. Unlike grasshoppers and crickets, which produce sound by rubbing together two body parts, such as two legs or a leg and wing, male cicadas produce sound in the thorax, the middle region of their bodies. In the last segment of the cicada's thorax, there are two hollow cavities covered on one side by membranes to which strong muscles are attached. Sound waves are generated when the muscles vibrate the membranes at a high frequency. The fact that most of the cicada's large abdomen is empty may help amplify the sounds produced in the thorax.*

The male cicadas' singing attracts other males to the same spot, stimulating them to sing as well, and often resulting in the gathering of a large number of males in the same trees, all of them singing at once (thereby creating Paul Fleischman's "joyful noise").

The males' singing, in turn, attracts female cicadas who choose males and mate. Each species has its own distinct song, which is used to help species find appropriate mates. Further, each species sings at a particular time of day—some sing in the middle of the day, some in the evening—and often in its own particular habitat.

Habitat: *Cicadas are generally found in areas of tall shade trees. They are common in many suburban areas in North America.*

Life Cycle: *Once cicadas have mated, the females lay their eggs in slits they have made in the bark of young twigs of trees. After about six weeks the eggs hatch and the nymphs fall to the ground and begin immediately to dig down toward the roots, where they feed. The nymphs remain underground for 1 to 17 years (2 to 5 years in most species), gradually maturing in tunnels they have created. When they are ready to emerge, in summer, the nymphs tunnel up to the surface and climb up the nearest trees The adult cicada emerges through a split in the top of the nymphal skin.*

Materials

Computers and database or hypermedia software

Materials

Tape recorder and blank audio-tape for each cooperative group of four to five

As an alternative to completing the written portions of the activity sheet, if computers and appropriate database or hypermedia software are available, encourage the students to add to their insect databases or hypermedia stacks or folders. (A listing of appropriate database fields is provided in descriptions of this activity for use with poems that appear earlier in Fleischman's collection.)

4. Taking a Sound Field Trip. Invite the students to collect joyful noises. Suggest that they conduct field trips in and around school and in their homes and neighborhoods to collect sounds they love to hear.

Supply each group of four or five students with a tape recorder and a blank audiocassette tape. Tell them to work together to record as many joyful noises as they can gather in and around school. Suggest that each day after school, one of the group members take the tape recorder and cassette home to record joyful noises in his or her neighborhood and home.

When each group has completed its sound field trip, have it prepare an oral presentation of the sounds collected. Encourage the group to have each member take part in the presentation, explaining sounds he or she collected and why those sounds are joyful noises. Consider combining this activity with the poetry writing idea described above by giving students an opportunity to prepare audio accompaniments to their joyful noise poems.

5. A Joyful Mood. Provide the students with a variety of materials with which they can create color illustrations, such as colored felt-tip markers, chalks and oil pastels in a variety of colors, and drawing paper. Encourage them to choose a medium with which they are comfortable.

Then invite the students to listen to recordings of joyful music. You might, for example, play a recording of the *Hallelujah!* chorus from Handel's oratorio *Messiah,* a portion of the Finale of Beethoven's Ninth Symphony, Telemann's "Réjouissance" from the *Suite in A minor for Flute and Strings,* selections from Aaron Copland's *El Salón México* or *Rodeo,* or the festive dancing rhythms of the opening Allegro of the concerto "Autumn" from Vivaldi's *The Four Seasons.* Or you might invite students to bring to class recorded musical selections of joyful music. Encourage the students to listen closely to the music and then to express through their drawings or paintings how the music makes them feel.

Tell the students they may create *objective* or *nonobjective* pictures, that is, their illustrations may show objects or scenes or they may communicate ideas or feelings solely through use of color, line, light, and so on.

Give students appropriate space in which to complete their illustrations and sufficient time and encouragement to do so.

When they have completed their work, have them share with the class the moods they have tried to express in their creations and the manner in which they used color, line, and light to do so. Encourage them to post their work in the classroom, if they choose to do so.

6. How is Sound Produced? Recall with the students how cicadas produce sound: In the last segment of the cicada's thorax there are two hollow cavities, each covered on one side by a membrane to which a strong muscle is attached. The cicada generates sound waves when the muscles vibrate the membranes at a high frequency. The fact that most of the cicada's large abdomen is empty may help amplify the sounds produced in the thorax.

Demonstrate for the students how sound is produced by vibrating objects. Here are some ways to do so:

- Place a yardstick (or meter stick) on a table with half of it extending over the table's edge and the other half held firmly to the table. Push downward on the edge of the half hanging over the table and release it. Have the students observe and listen closely to what happens. Move the yardstick so a different length extends over the edge and repeat the activity. Do so several times. Ask the students to explain what they have observed: As the length of the yardstick hanging over the edge is decreased, the speed of the vibration increases and the pitch of the sound goes up.

- Make a small hole in one end of a 12-inch wooden ruler or a thin piece of wood of the same length. Tie a piece of strong string tightly through the hole and swing the ruler in a circle at a steady rate fast enough to produce sound. Have the students observe and listen carefully to what

Materials

Markers, chalks, and oil pastels in a variety of colors

Drawing paper

Soft tissues (to blend chalks)

Sponge (to dampen drawing paper if chalks are used)

Damp paper towels (to clean hands and desk- or tabletops)

Smocks for students

Newspapers (to cover desks or tables)

Recorded selections of joyful music

Appropriate playback equipment

Materials

Yardstick (or meter stick)

12 in. wooden ruler, or thin piece of wood of the same size, and strong string

Medium-sized tin can or cylindrical cardboard oatmeal container; rubber balloon or sheet; salt; sharpened pencil; rubber stopper or solid rubber ball happens. Increase the rate at which you swing the ruler. Ask the students to explain what they have observed: As the ruler is swung more quickly, or harder, the more it vibrates and the louder the sound it produces.

■ Carefully remove both ends of a medium-sized tin can or cylindrical cardboard oatmeal container. Stretch one thickness of a rubber balloon or sheet tightly over one end of the container and fasten it with string or a strong rubber band. Make a rubber hammer by inserting the sharpened end of a pencil into a rubber stopper or small, solid rubber ball. Strike the drum you have created and have the students observe and listen carefully. Strike it again, harder, and ask the students to explain what they have observed: As the drum is struck with greater force, the drum skin vibrates more rapidly and produces a louder sound.

Strike the drum repeatedly, giving each student an opportunity to feel the vibrations. Tell them you will give them an opportunity to see the vibrations. Sprinkle salt on the drum skin and tap it. Have the students observe what happens. Strike the drum head harder. Ask the students to explain what they have observed: The salt forms a pattern created by the vibrations and the pattern changes as the drum is struck harder.

Keep the drum flat with the salt still on the drum skin. Shout into the open end of the drum. Have the students observe what happens. Vary the pitch and loudness of your shouting. Ask the students to explain what they observe: The pattern of the salt is altered by the pitch and loudness of the shouting.

Challenge the students to devise similar demonstrations of sound produced by vibrating objects. Explain that whether we hear sounds depends upon the number of vibrations that are produced. An object must vibrate at least 16 times per second to produce audible sounds, but vibrations above 20,000 per second are inaudible by humans.

If time permits, use this opportunity to explore the phenomenon of sound with the students. Encourage them to do research— individually, in pairs, or in small cooperative groups—to determine and then demonstrate such phenomena as how sound travels, what materials carry sound waves, and how we make music with sounds.

Before the Reading

Prepare your students to read Paul Fleischman's poem "Honeybees" by using one or both of the following suggestions:

1. Ask the students whether they belong to any groups or associations with other people. Summarize their responses on the chalkboard. Ask them whether they think it fair to conclude that since they belong to particular groups, they are exactly the same as other members of those groups, that is, that they have the same values, outlooks, personalities, and so on. Ask them to explain their responses and to make their explanations concrete by giving specific examples.

Tell the students they will shortly listen to and read a poem in which Paul Fleischman humorously reminds us that all members of the same groups do not necessarily see things in quite the same way. Encourage them to listen carefully to find out which group the poet uses to make his point.

2. Ask the students what their favorite activities or pastimes are. List them on the chalkboard. Then ask if there are any students who do not like any of the activities or pastimes listed. Ask them to explain why. Ask the students who suggested that they be listed to explain what they like about them. Point out that even though everyone in the class shares a number of characteristics—all are human beings, all are students, all are members of a particular class who live in a particular place, and so on—not everyone sees things in quite the same way. Not everyone has the same point of view.

Tell the students they will soon listen to and read an amusing poem in which Paul Fleischman describes how two insects from the same family, genus, and species have remarkably different points of view. Encourage them to listen carefully to discover which insect he describes and how different the two representatives of the species are from each other.

During the Reading

Materials

Teacher copy of *Joyful Noise*

Tape recorder and prerecorded version of "Honeybees" (optional; a cassette tape, *Joyful Noise and I Am Phoenix, Poems for Two Voices,* by Paul Fleischman, performed by John Bedford Lloyd and Anne Twomey, available from Harper & Row)

Copy of *Joyful Noise* for student reader (optional)

1. Have the students listen as you play for them a reading of "Honeybees" that you and a colleague have recorded on audiotape in advance of the class. Alternatively, play the recording of the poem available on cassette tape from Harper & Row, publishers of *Joyful Noise.* Or, prior to class, carefully prepare to read the poem to them along with one of your students, you taking the left-hand part and the student the right-hand part.

Set the stage for your reading or tape playback by helping your students focus their attention on the poem. Ask them to imagine how tired and bored or frustrated they became after a long period of hard work that they did not enjoy and that did not seem to be appreciated by those who benefited from it. Then ask them to imagine what it would have taken to make them feel just the opposite—relaxed, comfortable, and successful.

Play the prerecorded version of the poem or read the poem to the students. Read with appropriate expression to help the students apply their imaginations to the poem. Help them appreciate the strikingly different points of view of the worker bee and the queen bee.

Materials

Student copies of *Joyful Noise*

Tape recorder and prerecorded version of "Honeybees" (optional)

Materials

Student copies of *Joyful Noise*

Tape recorders for use by student pairs

Materials

Students' personal dictionaries

After the Reading

Materials

Writing paper; pens or pencils

2. Distribute copies of *Joyful Noise* to the students and have them follow in their copies as you play for them once again the prerecorded version of "Honeybees" or as you re-read the poem together with the student with whom you practiced.

Ask the students what they pictured in their minds as they listened to "Honeybees." Ask them with which of the two bees they most easily identified themselves, and why.

3. Allow the students to read "Honeybees" again, silently. Then pair students and ask each pair to practice reading the poem, or selected portions of it, together. Tell both readers to read from top to bottom, one taking the left-hand part, the other the right-hand part, and both speaking at the same time all lines printed on the same horizontal level.

Give pairs opportunities to record and play back their readings to help them achieve a smooth presentation of the poem. When they are ready, have them read the poem or selected portion to the class or to a small group within the class. Or they may play back a recording they have made of the reading.

Pair students who have difficulty with this oral presentation with more skilled students. Assist pairs as needed.

4. Have students add to their personal dictionaries any unfamiliar words they encounter in "Honeybees." Encourage them to seek from other students—reading partners, cooperative group members, and so on—suggestions about the meanings and pronunciations of the words. If you have distributed copies of the Glossary, encourage them to look up the meanings of the words and terms.

1. Poetry Idea: Points of View. Ask students to suggest groups or categories to which two people may belong who nevertheless have strikingly different points of view about the same thing. Two students in the same class, for example, might feel differently about the class: One may enjoy it immensely and the other might find it a bore. One music lover might find classical music easy to listen to, even stimulating, whereas another might find it stuffy or artificial. Two book lovers might have notably different tastes in books: One might like mystery novels whereas the other might consider reading such novels a waste of time, preferring biographies instead.

Summarize the students' suggestions on the chalkboard. Then pair the students or invite them to choose partners. Encourage the partners to collaborate on a poem in which they describe two quite different points of view about the same thing or experience. Suggest they begin their poems somewhat like Paul Fleischman begins "Honeybees." For example:

Being a student

is a drag.

I like to work with my hands
and love
to make things work.
Let me explain.

My teachers ignore me.
I fidget in my seat,
bored by their words. ...

Being a student
is a lot of fun.

I like to learn from books
and love to talk
and listen.

Let me explain.
My teachers like me.
I pay close attention
to what they say.

Answer any questions the students may have about this poetry idea. Solicit additional ideas from them. Tell them they might write serious poems or humorous poems—or a combination of the two.

When you are sure the students understand the instructions, encourage them to begin writing. Circulate among them and offer assistance.

Encourage the student pairs to share with other pairs their work in progress. Have pairs who complete their poems quickly work together with pairs who are having difficulty, or have them write an additional "Points of View" poem.

When the student pairs have completed their poems, invite them to read them aloud to the class. Respond enthusiastically and seek clarification when necessary. Post the students' poems in the classroom for all to read. Save the poems you have posted, as possible contributions to a book of student poetry to be compiled when the poetry teaching unit has been completed.

Materials

Activity Sheet 1 (one per student, pair or cooperative group)

Printed resources about insects

Pens or pencils; drawing instruments

2. What Do You Know About Honeybees? Ask how many students have ever seen a honeybee. Ask those who have to describe the settings in which they have seen honeybees. Ask: What does a honeybee look like? What was it doing when you saw it? When can honeybees generally be seen?

Point out that honeybees are commonly seen in summer around large patches of flowers, especially on warm, sunny days.

Distribute to the students copies of Activity Sheet 1. Provide them with or guide them to resources they may use to gather information about honeybees so they may complete the activity sheet. (See the Recommended Reading and Audiovisual Resources and Biological Supply Houses lists at the end of the literature teaching guide. Encyclopedias and books on general biology or the life sciences may also provide information to help students complete the activity sheet.)

In addition, if time of year and location are appropriate, encourage the students to gather as much information about honeybees as they can simply by observing the insects in their natural habitats. Since it may be dangerous to attempt to capture honeybees, do not recommend that students attempt to do so, as they have done with some other insects.

Allow students to conduct their research and field observations individually, with partners, or in small groups of three or four students. Remind them that each member of a pair or cooperative group should be prepared to demonstrate the tasks each performed and that all students should be able to explain any of the information provided on the completed activity sheet.

When the students have completed their activity sheets, invite them to report to their classmates the information they have gathered. If information provided by students differs, have them cite their sources of information—printed materials, audiovisual resources, and field observations—and try to determine why there are differences among the reports. Finally, have the individual students, pairs, or cooperative groups keep the activity sheets they have prepared on honeybees to combine in a class publication with similar activity sheets on the other insects featured in the poems of *Joyful Noise*.

FOR THE TEACHER

Insect Name: *Honeybee*

Phylum: *Arthropoda*

Class: *Insecta*

Order: *Hymenoptera*

Family: *Apidae*

General Physical Characteristics: *There are three classes, or forms, of honeybee, each exhibiting somewhat different physical characteristics. In all three classes, the thorax is hairy and brownish, and the abdomen banded in dull orange or gold and black.*

All three forms live together in colonies, in a highly developed social organization, for which the honeycomb serves as the structural base.

The queen is the largest of the three forms. Rarely seen, she has a long abdomen and a sting which she uses only to fight rival queens.

The drone is the next largest in size. He has large eyes that meet at the top of his head and has no sting.

The worker is the smallest and by far the most numerous of the honeybee forms. All workers are sterile females. They range in body length from 3/8 to 5/8 inches. Workers have compound eyes on either side of the head with three single eyes between them. Their two antennae carry thousands of tiny spots that function as organs of smell and hearing. They have two pairs of wings, the smaller of which is folded under the larger when the bees are at rest. Their six legs are equipped with a variety of tools—combs, brushes, scrapers, and nippers—which they use to perform a number of functions. In addition, their hindlegs are equipped with pollen baskets for storing the pollen they gather from flowers.

Workers carry their stings on their abdomens and use them for defense. Each sting is composed of two slender shafts, each notched with barbs. A worker can use her sting only once; she dies when the barbed shafts are torn from her body.

100

Typical Behavior: *The queen performs no other nest function than egg laying. Queens may live for several seasons.*

The strongest or most active of the drones, which are comparatively few in number in any nest, mates with the queen in mid-air, after which it tumbles to the ground and dies. The remaining drones are ejected from the nest at the end of summer, after which they die, having no further function in the social organization. In summer, drones live about eight weeks.

The workers perform a remarkable variety and number of functions, only some of which are apparent outside the nest and most of which are related to the age of the workers, which may live only about six weeks in summer. Workers spend their first days tidying the nest, or honeycomb, repairing it, smoothing its rough walls, and fastening it into place with propolis, or bee glue, which they scrape from the buds of trees and carry back to the honeycomb in their pollen baskets.

Once they have learned to use their wings, they begin gathering nectar, the sweet liquid secreted by various flowers, which is changed into honey in the workers' honey sacs. They also gather pollen, which they carry back to the honeycomb in their pollen baskets. Some of the pollen is rubbed off onto other flowers than those from which it was initially gathered, causing cross-pollination and thus permitting flower species to survive changes in the environment. Although the workers' gathering trips may encompass four or five miles, generally the workers do not range more than a half mile from the honeycomb.

When workers find sources of nectar, they return to the nest and, through a series of dance-like movements on the comb, communicate to other workers the location of the nectar source. The other workers then make a "beeline" between the comb and the food source.

Once they complete their gathering and return to the honeycomb, the workers empty the contents of their honey sacs into the cells of the comb, where it ripens, and empty the pollen into other cells.

The workers consume the honey, from which they produce wax in flakes from glands between the joints of their abdomens. They then chew the wax, mixing it with saliva, and spread it in thin bands, shaping it into six-sided cells, which make up the honeycomb. Some of the cells are destined as storage places for honey and pollen, others as brood cells for the eggs laid by the queen bee. Brood cells vary in size according to the class of bee that will develop in them. Worker cells are relatively small, drone cells larger, and queen bee cells the largest of all.

Workers also serve as nursemaids to newly hatched bee grubs, feeding them first with royal jelly, a special saliva that they produce, then with honey and beebread, a mixture of pollen with nectar and honey. Future queens, whose eggs have been laid in larger cells, are fed with royal jelly alone.

Finally, workers serve as guards at the nest entrance. When danger approaches, they secrete a pheromone—a chemical that causes a reaction

101

in other individuals of the same species—at the base of their sting apparatus, which brings other workers to the point of danger.

Habitat: *Honeybees may be found throughout North America, with the exception of the Far North, generally in gardens, fields, orchards, croplands, and woodlands.*

Life Cycle: *When a nest becomes too crowded, generally in late spring or summer, the queen bee decides to seek a new home. She leaves the nest accompanied in a swarm by most of the worker bees. The swarm settles in a cluster around the queen, while some workers seek out a new nest site and construct a new honeycomb.*

In the former nest a daughter queen emerges from her brood cell and goes immediately to other brood cells to sting younger queens to death. She then leaves the nest and flies straight upward, followed by the drones, one of which overtakes her, mates with her in mid-air, and then falls to the ground and dies.

The queen then crawls back into the nest ready to lay eggs. She lays a single egg in each brood cell, and sometimes more than 1,000 eggs a day. In most cells she lays fertile eggs, which will develop into workers or queens. In a few she lays infertile eggs, which will develop into drones.

In about three days the eggs hatch into tiny grubs, or larvae. At first, all of them are fed by workers on royal jelly. Later, larvae destined to become workers have honey and beebread added to their menu. The larvae mature in about six days. Then their brood cells are covered over by workers with a porous wax cap, and the larvae enter the pupal stage. In 12 to 14 days, full-grown workers gnaw their ways out of their cells, ready to begin their brief lives of toil.

Larvae destined to become queens are stuffed with royal jelly. In about 16 days they become full-fledged queens.

Materials

Computers and database or hypermedia software

Materials

Writing paper and pencils or pens for each pair

Student copies of *Joyful Noise*

As an alternative to completing the written portions of the activity sheet, if computers and appropriate database hypermedia software are available, encourage the students to add to their insect databases or hypermedia stacks or folders. (A listing of appropriate database fields is provided in descriptions of this activity for use with poems that appear earlier in Fleischman's collection.)

3. Active and Passive. Use Paul Fleischman's poem "Honeybees" to explore or review the active and passive voices with the students. Pair the students and provide each pair with a piece of paper and pencils or pens. Ask the pairs to divide the sheet of paper into two columns. In the first column have them list all the verbs and verb forms used by the worker bee after the first four lines. Thus, *am, guarding, take, put, making,* etc.

In the second column have them list all the verbs and verb forms used by the queen bee after the first four lines. Thus, *rising, am fed, am bathed, am groomed,* etc.

When the student pairs have completed their task, ask volunteers to share their lists with the class. Record their findings on the chalkboard, and ask class members to add to or subtract from the chalkboard lists based on their own findings. Then add to or subtract from the lists, as you clarify what verbs are *(words, or parts of speech, that express action, occurrence, or existence)*.

Next ask the students to compare the two lists. Ask what they find different about them. If no student suggests it, point out that most of the verbs used by the worker bee express action: They describe the worker *doing* something, such as guarding the nest, taking out the trash, making wax, collecting nectar, and so on. Then point out that most of the verbs used by the queen describe her having something *done to* or *for* her, such as being fed, being bathed, being groomed, and so on.

Ask if anyone knows what those differences are called. Explain that when the subject of the verb—in the first list, the worker bee—is the *doer* of the action, the verb is in the *active voice*. Explain that when the subject of the verb—in the second list, the queen bee—is the *receiver* or *undergoer* of the action of the verb, the verb is in the *passive voice*.

Check the students' understanding of active and passive voice by having the pairs examine the poem "Water Striders" and list in two columns all the examples of active and passive voice they can find. Have them share their findings with the class and invite class members to add to or subtract from the lists. Offer explanation and correction as needed.

Conclude by asking the students whether they think it better to be active or passive and why they think that way. Point out that the queen bee, by living a basically passive existence in which almost everything is done for her, loses the ability to forage, that is, to find food for herself. She becomes dependent on the workers to provide for her. Ask whether they think humans can become too dependent if they live passive lives.

Materials

Long, thick rope

Stationary object on a grassy field (a boulder or tree stump)

Gloves for students

4. Strength in Numbers. Recall with the students the worker bee's wonderment that all the workers bees had not "unionized." Ask the students what they think she means by that.

Discover what the students know of labor unions and why unions are formed. Provide examples of labor unions and other associations (Chambers of Commerce, Neighborhood Watch programs, political parties, and so on) created to strengthen the influence or ability of their individual members. Elicit other examples from the students.

Write the following statement on the chalkboard: "In numbers there is strength." Ask how that saying applies to the unions and other associations you have described and students have suggested. Ask for other examples of the accuracy of the saying.

Tell the students there are many physical activities in which the saying also holds true. Ask for a volunteer student who thinks he or she is especially strong. Hand the student a single sheet of paper and ask him or her to tear it in half. When the student has done so, hand him or her a large telephone directory or similar book of substantial size and ask the student to tear it in half in the same way (not page-by-page, but all at once). Allow other students to try their hand. Then ask how the saying on the chalkboard might be said to apply to this situation.

Tell the students you will give them an opportunity to play a game in which they can demonstrate the accuracy of the saying. The game is best

103

played outdoors, on soft grass. You will need a long, sturdy rope and a stationary object, such as a large boulder or tree stump. Ask for a student volunteer. The larger and stronger the student is, the more clearly you will be able to demonstrate the accuracy of the saying.

Have the volunteer station himself or herself behind the stationary object and wrap the rope behind his or her back and under his or her arms. Extra padding under the rope will assure that the volunteer does not suffer any rope burns. Then have the volunteer prop his or her feet against the object. Invite a second volunteer to come forward, take the ends of the rope, and try to pull the first student straight up and out from behind the object. (Provide gloves to prevent rope burns.) If that proves impossible, ask for a second student volunteer to help pull, and so on, until the pullers are successful.

Give all the students opportunities to take part as pullers and pulled. Have them keep track of the number of students it takes in each instance to pull the single student straight up and out from behind the object.

Ask them if they can think of other physical endeavors, including games, in which there is strength in numbers. Ask if they can think of examples of the saying's accuracy in undertakings that do not involve or require heavy physical exertion.

WHIRLIGIG BEETLES

Before the Reading

Prepare your students to read Paul Fleischman's poem "Whirligig Beetles" by using one or both of the following suggestions:

1. Ask if any students have ever gone on a vacation or trip. Invite them to state their vacation or trip destinations. Record the destinations on the chalkboard or invite a student volunteer to do so. Then ask the students how they traveled to their destinations, what they did along the way, and whether they enjoyed their travel. Ask if anyone has ever had the experience of enjoying the travel as much as or more than the destination. Encourage them to explain why.

Tell the students they are about to listen to and read a poem in which Paul Fleischman describes an insect that apparently gets more pleasure out of traveling than arriving. Encourage them to listen carefully to find out what insect he describes and how the insect travels.

2. Draw two points on the chalkboard, separated from each other by at least 4 feet. Ask the students to indicate the shortest distance between the two points. If any students suggest an answer other than a straight line, measure the distances suggested to determine which is the shortest.

Once the students have agreed that the shortest distance is a straight line, ask them whether they think the shortest route is always the best route from one place to another. Ask for examples of situations in which longer routes may be preferable to the shortest one.

Tell them they are about to listen to and read a poem in which the most roundabout, indirect route is presented as the best possible route. Encourage them to listen carefully to see if they agree.

During the Reading

Materials

Teacher copy of *Joyful Noise*

Tape recorder and prerecorded version of "Whirligig Beetles" (optional; a cassette tape, *Joyful Noise and I Am Phoenix, Poems for Two Voices*, by Paul Fleischman, performed by John Bedford Lloyd and Anne Twomey, available from Harper & Row)

Copy of *Joyful Noise* for student reader (optional)

1. Have the students listen as you play for them a reading of "Whirligig Beetles" that you and a colleague have recorded on audiotape in advance of the class. Alternatively, play the recording of the poem available on cassette tape from Harper & Row, publishers of *Joyful Noise*. Or, prior to class, carefully prepare to read the poem to them along with one of your students, you taking the left-hand part and the student the right-hand part.

Set the stage for your reading or tape playback by helping your students focus their attention on the poem. Ask them to think about physical movements or motions they perform for the sheer pleasure of it, such as dancing, running, hiking, and swimming.

Play the prerecorded version of the poem or read the poem to the students. Read with appropriate expression to help the students apply their imaginations to the poem. Help them visualize the continuous spinning, swerving, weaving, whirling movement of the whirligig beetles the poet describes.

Materials

Student copies of *Joyful Noise*

Tape recorder and prerecorded version of "Whirligig Beetles" (optional)

Materials

Student copies of *Joyful Noise*

Tape recorders for use by student pairs

Materials

Students' personal dictionaries

After the Reading

Materials

Activity Sheet 1 (one per student, pair, or cooperative group)

Pens or pencils; drawing instruments

Printed resources about insects

Two-handled seines (optional; see Activity Sheet 3; one per student, pair, or cooperative group)

Clear glass, wide-mouthed jars (optional)

10-power magnifying glass (optional)

Rectangular aquariums, sand, water, green plants (optional)

2. Distribute copies of *Joyful Noise* to the students and have them follow in their copies as you play for them once again the prerecorded version of "Whirligig Beetles" or as you reread the poem together with the student with whom you practiced.

Ask the students what they pictured in their minds as they listened to "Whirligig Beetles." Ask if they were able to imagine the sort of movement the beetles appear to enjoy so much.

3. Allow the students to read "Whirligig Beetles" again, silently. Then pair students and ask each pair to practice reading the poem, or selected portions of it, together. Tell both readers to read from top to bottom, one taking the left-hand part, the other the right-hand part, and both speaking at the same time all lines printed on the same horizontal level.

Give pairs opportunities to record and play back their readings to help them achieve a smooth presentation of the poem. When they are ready, have them read the poem or selected portion to the class or to a small group within the class. Or they may play back a recording they have made of their reading.

Pair students who have difficulty with this oral presentation with more skilled students. Assist pairs as needed.

4. Have students add to their personal dictionaries any unfamiliar words they encounter in "Whirligig Beetles." Encourage them to seek from other students—reading partners, cooperative group members, and so on—suggestions about the meanings and pronunciations of the words. If you have distributed copies of the Glossary, encourage them to look up the meanings of the words and terms.

1. What Do You Know About Whirligig Beetles? Ask how many students have ever seen a whirligig beetle. Ask those who have to describe the settings in which they have seen it. Ask: What does a whirligig beetle look like? How does it move? When can whirligig beetles generally be seen?

Point out that whirligig beetles are commonly seen on warm days, especially in spring, on the surface of lakes, ponds, and quiet pools in streams.

Distribute to the students copies of Activity Sheet 1. Provide them with or guide them to resources they may use to gather information about whirligig beetles so they may complete the activity sheet. (See the Recommended Reading and Audiovisual Resources and Biological Supply Houses lists at the end of the literature teaching guide. Encyclopedias and books on general biology or the life sciences may also provide information to help students complete the activity sheet.)

In addition, if time of year and location are appropriate, encourage the students to gather as much information about whirligig beetles as they can simply by observing the insects in their natural habitats. Suggest that they make two-handled seines to collect specimens for observation. (See Activity Sheet 3.)

Tell the students that with care and quick reflexes they may be able to capture whirligig beetles in the seines and transfer them to clear glass, wide-mouthed jars so they can observe the insect closely. Tell them to punch holes in the jar lids and to put a little water in the jars along with some vegetation and perhaps some small insects. Remind them that they might also find a magnifying glass helpful in observing the details of the whirligig beetle's structure and coloring. Finally, tell your students to be sure to return the whirligig beetles to their natural habitat when their observations have been completed.

As an adjunct or alternative to observations that individual students conduct of whirligig beetles in their natural habitats, arrange for students to conduct observations in the classroom setting. Have one or more students capture whirligig beetles, in the manner described, and bring them to the classroom. Or check to see whether live specimens are available from one of the biological supply houses listed at the end of this teaching guide. Place the whirligig beetles in rectangular aquariums with about an inch of clean sand at the bottom and two-thirds full of water. Add several green plants anchoring them at the bottom with stones. Furnish the aquariums with small insects as food for the beetles. Cover the aquarium with fine mesh netting.

Encourage the students to observe and record the physical characteristics of the whirligig beetles, their eating habits, and so on. Encourage them to use the beetles as models for illustrations they make on their activity sheets.

Allow students to conduct their research and field observations individually, with partners, or in small groups of three or four students. Remind them that each member of a pair or cooperative group should be prepared to demonstrate the tasks each performed and that all students should be able to explain any of the information provided on the completed activity sheet.

When the students have completed their activity sheets, invite them to report to their classmates the information they have gathered. If information provided by students differs, have them cite their sources of information—printed materials, audiovisual resources, and field observations—and try to determine why there are differences among the reports. Finally, have the individual students, pairs, or cooperative groups keep the activity sheets they have prepared on whirligig beetles to combine in a class publication with similar activity sheets on the other insects featured in the poems of *Joyful Noise*.

FOR THE TEACHER

Insect Name: *Whirligig Beetle*

Phylum: *Arthropoda*

Class: *Insecta*

Order: *Coleoptera*

Family: *Gyrinidae*

General Physical Characteristics: *Adult whirligig beetles are elongate-oval and somewhat flattened in shape and blue-black or dark bronze in color. They have long, slender front legs, suited for grasping prey on the water, and shorter, paddlelike middle and hindlegs, which are adapted for swimming.*

Whirligig beetles swim with half their bodies above the water and half below. In order to see predators both above and below the water line, these beetles have undergone a remarkable adaptation. Each of their eyes is separated into two parts: the top portion is adapted for sight above the water and the bottom portion for sight below the water.

Whirligig beetles possess sensitive antennae by which they detect changes in the ripples on the surface of the water, thus allowing them to tell where other beetles are as well as where other insects, struggling on the water surface, might be found.

There are two genera of whirligig beetles, Dineutas and Gyrinus. The adult body length of beetles of the Dineutas family is about 3/8 to 5/8 of an inch; the body length of adult beetles in the Gyrinus family is about 1/8 to 1/4 of an inch.

Typical Behavior: *Whirligig beetles have often been compared in appearance to watermelon seeds or coffee beans resting on the water's surface. Once they are disturbed, however, they begin to mill around rapidly in the continuous movement for which they are named. They whirl in tight arcs about one another, but without hitting one another. The movement apparently is a defense mechanism to confuse predators.*

Many species of whirligig beetle exude a milky secretion whose odor often is compared to the scent of apples or of vanilla. These beetles are sometimes called "apple smellers" or "vanilla bugs."

Many species have wings and are able to fly, though they appear to prefer staying on the water.

Adult whirligig beetles are scavengers, feeding on insects that have fallen onto the surface of the water and on worms and small vertebrates. Whirligig larvae feed on aquatic insects and mites which they chase down.

Habitat: *Whirligig beetles are commonly found on the surfaces of quiet, shady pools and ponds, the coves of lakes, and the backwaters of rivers and streams.*

Life Cycle: *In early spring adult whirligig beetles mate. The female lays its eggs in rows or clusters on the stems of submerged foliage and then dies. The eggs hatch in about two weeks, and for the next two or three months the whirligig beetle larvae remain underwater, feeding on insects and other small animals which they find in the debris at the bottom of the water.*

Mature larvae crawl up onto the water's bank where they construct their pupal cases from various materials, often dirt mixed with saliva. They remain in the pupal stage for about a week, after which they emerge as new adults in mid to late summer. Generally they form aggregations on the water. In fall, they leave the surface and overwinter in the mud or on plants.

Whirligig beetles produce a single generation each year.

Materials

Computers and database or hypermedia software

Materials

Writing paper; pens or pencils

As an alternative to completing the written portions of the activity sheet, if computers and appropriate database or hypermedia software are available, encourage the students to add to their insect databases or hypermedia stacks or folders. (A listing of appropriate database fields is provided in descriptions of this activity for use with poems that appear earlier in Fleischman's collection.)

2. Poetry Idea: "Eyes in the Back of My Head" Remind the students of the remarkable adaptation whirligig beetles have undergone that permits them to see above and below the water line at the same time. Ask why this adaptation has taken place. (Apparently it permits whirligig beetles to see predators both above and below the water line.) Ask if they are aware of other adaptations in the animal world that permit specific animals to function effectively or to protect themselves. (The coloring of some animals, for example, allows them to blend in with their surroundings and thus avoid easy detection by predators.)

Ask the students to imagine what it would be like if they underwent a physical transformation by which they had not only the eyes they now possess but also eyes in the backs of their heads. Ask them to imagine what they could see that they do not now see and what they could do that they cannot now do.

Encourage the students to write poems in which they imagine they have eyes in the backs of their heads. Tell them to write about what they see in various places—the classroom, at home, at play with their friends, and so on—both from the front and from the back. Suggest they structure their poems using lines such as these: "When I am at home /I look to the front/And I see…/But when I look to the back/I see…."

Answer any questions the students may have about this poetry idea. If necessary, offer examples of the kinds of lines they might write. ("When I am at home eating dinner/I look to the front/And I see what I am eating/But when I look to the back/I see my favorite television show.") Solicit other examples from the students.

When you are sure the students understand the instructions, encourage them to begin writing. Circulate among them and offer assistance.

Encourage the students to share with one another their work in progress. Have those who complete their poems quickly work together with students who are having difficulty, or have them write an additional "Eyes in the Back of My Head" poem.

When the students have completed their poems, invite them to read them aloud to the class. Respond enthusiastically and seek clarification when necessary. Post the students' poems in the classroom for all to read. Save the poems you have posted, as possible contributions to a book of student poetry to be compiled when the poetry teaching unit has been completed.

Materials

Student copies of *Joyful Noise*

3. Circles, Spirals, Arcs, Ovals, and Loops. Have the students read "Whirligig Beetles" once again to determine the different shapes the poet says the beetles make as they move about. Ask them to list the shapes; record their suggestions on the chalkboard. The list should include circles, spirals, arcs, ovals, and loops.

Ask the students to explain each of the shapes listed by finding an example of it in the classroom. If no students are able to find classroom examples of one or another of the listed shapes, invite a volunteer student to draw the shape(s) on the chalkboard.

Ask the students to imagine what would happen if we were deprived of any of the shapes. They might conclude, for example, that if we were deprived of circles, our cars and trains would have no wheels, which exploit the geometrical properties of the circle. If we were deprived of ovals, eggs and footballs either would not exist or would have radically different shapes.

Tell the students you would like each of them to bring to class an example that occurs in nature of each of the listed shapes and a human-made example of each of the shapes. Tell the students that although the poem lists two-dimensional figures—figures considered according only to length and width—since all objects in nature exist in three dimensions—length, width, and thickness—the objects they bring will be three-dimensional. (If students have difficulty finding naturally occurring examples of the shapes, suggest that several flowers yield examples of circles and arcs, that some vines may provide loop formations, and that the spiral is evident in many forms of sea life, such as mollusca and shellfish, and in snail shells. Point out that eggs, as already noted, are oval in shape. Human-made examples of each of the shapes may be easier for the students to find.) Tell the students not to ignore the shapes represented by various parts of their bodies, such as their eyes, the half-moon arcs on their fingernails, and so on.

Give each student an opportunity to present the shapes he or she has found. Ask the other students whether the shapes presented demonstrate the appropriate qualities. Use this activity as an opportunity to review with students the characteristics of the geometric shapes and, if useful and applicable, the formulas used to measure them. Remind the students that the word *geometry* comes from a Greek word—*geometria*—which means *earth measurement*.

Materials

Appropriate music playback equipment

Student-provided music to accompany dancing

4. Dance, Dance, Dance. Ask the students to imagine the typical movement of whirligig beetles, as poet Paul Fleischman describes it, or to recall it as they saw it during their own observations. Ask if they can think of any situation in which groups of humans, if seen from above, might appear to be moving in somewhat the same manner, that is, moving in tight arcs, circles, ovals, loops, and spirals, not hitting or bumping into each other.

If no student mentions it, suggest that when humans dance for pleasure—when they engage in social dance—they might appear to be moving in similar fashion to whirligig beetles.

Ask students what their favorite dances are. Give them an opportunity to demonstrate and teach their favorite dances and dance steps to their classmates, using music they have selected. Provide appropriate music playback equipment and an appropriate space in the classroom or other available area. Encourage all students to take part—and take part yourself—either as teachers or students, or both.

Challenge groups of students to create a dance called "The Whirligig" in which their movements are patterned after those of the whirligig beetle. Allow them to select their own music and to choreograph steps, which they can demonstrate and teach other students.

Materials

Music metronome (optional)

5. Whirligiging. Recall with the students the remarkable ability of the whirligig beetles to move rapidly within their groups in continuous tight circles, arcs, ovals, loops, and spirals, without bumping into one another. Ask them to explain how the beetles can accomplish this feat: With their sensitive antennae they detect even slight changes in ripples on the surface of the water, allowing them to determine where other beetles are. (It may also be that the ripples from their own movements bounce back from objects in the water that the ripples hit and thus help the beetles to avoid hitting these objects.)

Tell the students you will give them an opportunity to "whirligig," that is, to play a game in which they have to move about rapidly without hitting others who also are moving about rapidly at the same time in the same area.

Select an area large enough for all the students to move freely at the same time—a gymnasium, or, if necessary, a classroom cleared of furniture and other obstacles. Pair the students and tell the students to begin moving about, hand in hand, in a slow walk within the area you have defined, without bumping into any other pairs. Have the students gradually increase the speed with which they move. It may help to use background music whose tempo increases gradually or a metronome, whose tempo you can increase.

When the game is over, ask the students what abilities they used to try to avoid bumping into each other. When students mention that they used their ability to see where they were going and where others were going, tell them, if they are responsible and trustworthy, that you will give them another opportunity to play the game, this time an eyes-shut version.

Have one partner in each pair shut his or her eyes and have the pairs repeat the process of moving, gradually more rapidly, in a defined area without bumping into anyone else. Tell the pairs they may use only hand signals of their own devising to communicate with each other about how to move, when to turn, when to stop and start, and so on. When the game is over, ask the students how they felt and have them compare playing the eyes-open and the eyes-shut versions of the game.

REQUIEM

Before the Reading

Prepare your students to read Paul Fleischman's poem "Requiem" by using one or both of the following suggestions:

1. Play for the students an audio recording of the Introit—the first item—of the Mass for the Dead, or *Requiem Mass,* in the Roman Catholic rites. If possible, obtain a recording of the selection in plainsong, although more elaborate musical settings of the Requiem Mass, such as those by Mozart, Verdi, and Berlioz, may be used instead.

Ask the students what they think of the music. Ask them how the music makes them feel. Ask if any students have ever heard such music.

Play the selection again. Then write the following initial words of the Introit in Latin on the chalkboard: *Requiem aeternam dona eis, Domine, et lux perpetua luceat eis.* Underneath, write this English translation of the Latin words: *"Grant them eternal rest, Lord, and let perpetual light shine upon them."*

Ask the students what they think the words mean and in what situation they might be used. Explain that the words are taken from the religious ceremonies commonly used in the Roman Catholic Church when a member of the church community has died and other members gather to pray for him or her just before burial.

Tell the students they are about to listen to and read a poem in which Paul Fleischman borrows the words from the initial part of the Requiem Mass. Encourage them to listen carefully to learn what he does with those words.

2. Ask if any students have participated in a funeral service or a memorial service for a family member or a friend who has died. Without requiring them to reveal more than they are comfortable revealing, ask students who have participated in such a service how it made them feel and what wishes or hopes they, or other participants, had for the person who died. Ask how those wishes or hopes were expressed at the service.

Tell the students they will shortly listen to and read a poem intended as a memorial following death. Ask them to listen carefully to determine who is being memorialized and what hopes are expressed for them.

During the Reading

Materials

Teacher copy of *Joyful Noise*

Tape recorder and prerecorded version of "Requiem" (optional; a cassette tape, *Joyful Noise and I Am Phoenix, Poems for Two Voices*, by Paul Fleischman, performed by John Bedford Lloyd and Anne Twomey, available from Harper & Row)

Recording of a Requiem Mass Introit (optional)

Copy of *Joyful Noise* for student reader (optional)

Materials

Student copies of *Joyful Noise*

Tape recorder and prerecorded version of "Requiem" (optional)

Materials

Student copies of *Joyful Noise*

Tape recorders for use by student pairs

Materials

Students' personal dictionaries

1. Have the students listen as you play for them a reading of "Requiem" that you and a colleague have recorded on audiotape in advance of the class. Alternatively, play the recording of the poem available on cassette tape from Harper & Row, publishers of *Joyful Noise*. Or, prior to class, prepare carefully to read the poem aloud along with one of your students, you taking the left-hand part and the student the right-hand part.

Set the stage for your reading or tape playback by helping your students focus their attention on the poem. Play a recording of the Introit to the Requiem Mass before you begin.

Then play the prerecorded version of the poem or read the poem to the students. Read with appropriate expression to help the students apply their imaginations to the poem.

2. Distribute copies of *Joyful Noise* to the students and have them follow in their copies as you play for them once again the prerecorded version of "Requiem" or as you re-read the poem together with the student with whom you practiced.

Ask the students what they pictured in their minds as they listened to "Requiem." Ask what mood the poem evokes in them.

3. Allow the students to read "Requiem" again, silently. Then pair students and ask each pair to practice reading the poem, or selected portions of it, together. Tell both readers to read from top to bottom, one taking the left-hand part, the other the right-hand part, and both speaking at the same time all lines printed on the same horizontal level.

Give pairs opportunities to record and play back their readings to help them achieve a smooth presentation of the poem. When they are ready, have them read the poem or selected portion to the class or to a small group within the class. Or they may play back a recording they have made of their reading.

Pair students who have difficulty with this oral presentation with students more skilled at it than they. Assist pairs as needed.

4. Have students add to their personal dictionaries any unfamiliar words they encounter in "Requiem." Encourage them to seek from other students—reading partners, cooperative group members, and so on—suggestions about the meanings and pronunciations of the words. If you have distributed copies of the Glossary, encourage them to look up the meanings of the words and terms.

After the Reading

Materials

Writing paper; pens or pencils

Materials

Activity Sheet 1 (one per student, pair, or cooperative group)

Printed resources about insects

Pens or pencils; drawing instruments

Sweeping nets (optional; see Activity Sheet 2)

Clear glass, wide-mouthed jars (optional)

10-power magnifying glass (optional)

1. **Poetry Idea: Eulogy.** Write the word *eulogy* in large letters on the chalkboard. Ask if any student knows what the word means. Explain that a eulogy is a speech or piece of writing meant to praise the virtues or accomplishments of a person, particularly someone who has died. Ask if any students have ever heard a eulogy, for example, at a funeral or memorial service. If appropriate, ask them to summarize what they heard.

Tell the students that it is not unusual for individuals to think about what they would want said of them after they die. Point out, for example, that two months before he was assassinated in April 1968, Dr. Martin Luther King, Jr., the American civil rights leader and Baptist minister, told his congregation what he hoped would be in his eulogy. He said that he would like somebody to mention "that Martin Luther King, Jr. tried to give his life serving others…that Martin Luther King, Jr. tried to love somebody."*

Invite the students to reflect on what they would like others to say about them after they die. Ask them to think about the most lasting impressions they would like to leave on other people.

Then invite the students to write poems in which they describe their desired eulogies. Help the students devise a form in which they can express their desires. You might suggest they borrow from Dr. King. Thus they might begin: "When I die/What would I want said of me?" Then they might continue: "I'd like somebody to say/That I…." Suggest that they repeat the two lines, each time indicating (as Dr. King did) another thing they would like said of them.

Answer any questions the students may have about this poetry idea. If necessary, offer examples of the kinds of lines they might write ("I'd like somebody to say/That I tried to help other people/I'd like somebody to say/That I always tried my best") Solicit other examples from the students.

When you are confident the students understand the instructions, encourage them to begin writing. Circulate among them and offer assistance.

Encourage the students to share with one another their work in progress. Have those who complete their poems quickly work together with students who are having difficulty, or have them write an additional "Eulogy" poem.

When the students have completed their poems, invite them to read them aloud to the class. Respond appreciatively and seek clarification when necessary. Post the students' poems in the classroom for all to read. Save the poems you have posted, as possible contributions to a book of student poetry to be compiled when the poetry teaching unit has been completed.

2. **What Do You Know About Mantises, Darners, Damselflies, and Katydids?** Have the students re-read "Requiem" and find the different kinds of insects mentioned in the poem. Then ask students to list the insects' names; record their list on the chalkboard.

---

*A written version of Dr. King's desired eulogy may be found in James Melvin Washington, ed. *A Testament of Hope: The Essential Writings of Martin Luther King, Jr.* (San Francisco: Harper & Row, 1986); see "The Drum Major Instinct," pp. 266–267. An audio recording of Dr. King's sermon is available on the following record album: *…Free at Last: Dr. Martin Luther King, Jr.* (Detroit, Michigan: Motown Record Corp., 1968; G929V1, Side 1, Band 2). It might be useful to play this selection for the students.

Ask which of the insects they have already learned about as they studied other poems in *Joyful Noise* (if the poems have been studied in the sequence in which Paul Fleischman presents them, the students have already learned about moths and grasshoppers in general and will next learn about one species of cricket). Underline the names of the remaining insects listed (praying mantises, darners, damselflies, and katydids), and ask how many students have ever seen any of them. Ask those who have to describe the settings in which they have seen them, what they look like, how they move about, and when, generally, they can be seen.

Distribute to the students copies of Activity Sheet 1. Tell them to choose one of the four types of insect underlined on the chalkboard. Provide them with or guide them to resources they may use to gather information about that insect so they may complete the activity sheet. (See the Recommended Reading and Audiovisual Resources and Biological Supply Houses lists at the end of the literature teaching guide. Encyclopedias and books on general biology or the life sciences may also provide information to help students complete the activity sheet.)

In addition, if time of year and location are appropriate, encourage the students to gather as much information about their chosen insect as they can simply by observing it in its natural habitat. Tell them that with care and quick reflexes they may be able to capture specimens of the insect in fine mesh sweeping nets (see Activity Sheet 2) and transfer them to clear glass, wide-mouthed jars with hole-punched lids so they can observe the specimens closely.

Tell them they might also find a magnifying glass (a ten-power glass is sufficient) helpful in observing the details of the insect's structure and coloring. Finally, tell your students to be sure to return the insect to its natural habitat when their observations have been completed.

As an adjunct or alternative to observations individual students conduct of their chosen insects in their natural habitats, arrange for students to conduct observations in the classroom setting. Have one or more students capture the insects, in the manner just described, and bring them to the classroom. Or check to see whether live specimens are available from one of the biological supply houses listed at the end of this teaching guide. Place the insects in terrariums or aquariums created by adding soil, plants, water, and food, as appropriate, to large, wide-mouthed jars placed on their sides. (Tell them to make sure the jar lids have air holes punched in them.) Encourage the students to observe and record the physical characteristics of the insects, their eating habits, and so on. Encourage them to use the insects as models for illustrations they make on their activity sheets.

Allow students to conduct their research and field observations individually, with partners, or in small groups of three or four students. Remind them that each member of a pair or cooperative group should be prepared to demonstrate the tasks each performed and that all students should be able to explain any of the information provided on the completed activity sheet.

When the students have completed their activity sheets, invite them to report to their classmates the information they have gathered. If information provided by students about the same insect differs, have them cite their sources of information—printed materials, audiovisual resources, and field observations—and try to determine why there are differences among the reports. Finally, have the individual students, pairs, or cooperative groups keep the activity sheets they have prepared to combine in a class publication with similar activity sheets on the other insects featured in the poems of *Joyful Noise*.

FOR THE TEACHER

Praying mantis: *These insects belong to the same order* (Orthoptera) *as grasshoppers, crickets, and katydids, and to the family* Mantidae. *They are large insects, ranging in size from 2 to 2 1/2 inches. They have protective green or brown coloring and a white spot under the base of each front leg. Their heads are triangular and their eyes bulge. Their front legs are enlarged and armed with spines for grasping prey.*

While hunting for prey, the mantis quietly holds its front legs folded in what appears to be a praying (preying?) position, from which it gets its name.

Praying mantises are commonly found in meadows, fields, and gardens in the Eastern United States and Southern Canada.

The female mantis lays its eggs in fall, gluing hundreds of them at a time in sticky masses to the stems and twigs of plants and even to buildings. The masses harden, forming a durable foam casing around the eggs. The nymphs hatch in late spring or early summer, and by late-summer they are full-grown and winged. The mantises then mate. The female kills the male, feeds on its body, and subsequently lays its eggs, as the life cycle is repeated. Mantises produce one generation per year.

Darners: *These insects belong to the order* Odonata, *the suborder* Anisoptera (Dragonflies), *and the family* Aeshnidae. *They are large, flying insects whose adult body length ranges from 2 3/4 to 3 inches, and whose wingspread may reach more than 4 inches. Their thoraxes may be green, brown, or blue, depending on the species. Their wings are clear.*

Male darners are quite territorial, patrolling their territories, often whole ponds, by flying 10 to 15 feet above the water and driving away any other male darners that enter their air space.

Darners may be found in ponds, marshes, and slow-moving streams throughout North America, particularly in the East.

Immediately after mating, the female lays her eggs, with the protective male hovering overhead. She deposits her eggs in the stems of aquatic plants. The darner naiads may remain in the water for more than a year, living among submerged vegetation and emerging as adults in the late spring or early summer.

Damselflies: *Like darners, damselflies belong to the order* Odonata. *They belong to the suborder* Zygoptera *and to a variety of families, including* Calopterygidae, Coenagrionidae, *and* Lestidae.

Damselflies are smaller and appear less sturdy than darners and other dragonflies. They are slender, almost delicate, with long, slim abdomens and small, broad heads with protruding eyes. Adult damselflies range in body length from 1 to 2 inches. Their coloring depends on their families and species as well as their sex. Their thoraxes and abdomens may be blue, green, red, gray, brown, or black. At rest, they hold their narrow wings over their bodies, or slightly fanned.

Damselflies live close to the surface of the water. Unlike dragonflies, they are not strong fliers, but they are skilled predators, feeding on small insects they capture in mid-flight.

They may be found throughout North America in ponds, marshes, and shallow streams.

Female damselflies deposit their eggs in aquatic plants above the water line, often while being held by their mates. The naiads overwinter in the water and emerge as adults the following year.

Katydids: *These insects belong to the same order as grasshoppers, crickets, and mantises* (Orthoptera) *and to the family* Tettigoniidae. *They range in adult body length from 1 to 2 1/2 inches. They are sometimes called longhorn grasshoppers. They are predominantly dark green in color, have long antennae and slender legs, and delicate wings that are heavily veined.*

Katydids are more frequently heard than seen. Their characteristic call, a shrill song—produced by males—interspersed with an occasional note that sounds like "Katy-she-did," gives them their name. They produce the song by rubbing together special roughened files at the base of their forewings. The call is a mating call that may be heard beginning in late July, occurring at dusk, and continuing until the first frost. As time passes, only the males who have failed to find mates continue calling.

Katydids may be found in forests, woodlands, and other stands of shade trees in many parts of North America, but especially in the Eastern United States and Southern Canada. They feed on foliage and, depending on the species, on stems, flowers, and the fruit of trees.

Katydids typically mate in the fall. In most cases the female inserts its eggs in the loose bark of twigs or on the edges of leaves. The eggs hatch the following spring. Katydids produce one generation per year.

Materials

Computers and database or hypermedia software

As an alternative to completing the written portions of the activity sheet, if computers and appropriate database or hypermedia software are available, encourage the students to add to their insect databases or hypermedia stacks or folders. (A listing of appropriate database fields is provided in descriptions of this activity for use with poems that appear earlier in Fleischman's collection.)

Materials

Crayons, markers, chalks in a variety of colors

Drawing paper for each student

Soft tissues (to blend chalks)

Sponge (to dampen paper, if chalks are used)

Damp paper towels (to clean hands and desktops or table tops)

Newspapers (to cover desks or tables)

3. What Color Do You Feel? Ask the students once again how the poem "Requiem" makes them feel. Record their answers on the chalkboard. Select other poems from *Joyful Noise* such as "Grasshoppers" and "Cicadas," and ask the students how those poems made them feel. Record their responses on the chalkboard.

Ask the students if they ever associate colors with their feelings. Tell them you will name a variety of feelings and ask them to respond with appropriate color names. Demonstrate what you mean by suggesting that you might say "angry," to which some individuals might respond "red," because that color suggests to them what being angry might look or feel like.

Ask the students to close their eyes and be still. Then tell them to say the colors they see as you name a variety of feelings. Name such feelings as sadness, hopefulness, joy, frustration, disappointment, satisfaction.

Next distribute crayons, colored markers and/or colored chalks and paper to the students and give them an opportunity to use color to express their feelings. Instruct them to

- use colors that make them feel happy to draw happy lines and shapes

- use colors that make them feel lonely to draw lonely lines or shapes

- use colors that make them feel hopeful to draw hopeful lines and shapes

- use colors that make them feel proud to draw proud lines and shapes

After each drawing session, invite the students to talk about the colors they chose and the shapes they drew.

Finally, tell the students to find colors that make them feel special or unique. Have them use those colors to draw their own special lines and shapes. Give students an opportunity to talk about their drawings. Display the completed drawings prominently in the classroom for all to see.

HOUSE CRICKETS

Before the Reading

Prepare your students to read Paul Fleischman's poem "House Crickets" by using one or both of the following suggestions:

1. Ask the students what their favorite seasons are. Ask what they especially like about those seasons. Ask them if there are things they enjoy doing during the typical weather of a particular season that they cannot do well or easily during other seasons. Summarize their responses on the chalkboard.

Tell the students they are about to listen to and read a poem about a particular kind of insect that appears to enjoy all the seasons and is not hindered or confined by any of them. Encourage them to listen carefully to find out what insect is described and how the insect is able to survive all the seasons equally well.

2. Ask the students if they have favorite foods that they identify with particular seasons of the year. List on the chalkboard the foods the students suggest, matching them with the appropriate seasons. Ask the students to explain why they think of particular foods when they think of particular seasons.

Tell them they will shortly listen to and read a poem in which an insect described by Paul Fleischman identifies the seasons of the year by particular kinds of food. Encourage them to listen carefully to discover what insect does that and by which foods it marks the change of seasons.

During the Reading

Materials

Teacher copy of *Joyful Noise*

Tape recorder and prerecorded version of "House Crickets" (optional; a cassette tape, *Joyful Noise and I Am Phoenix, Poems for Two Voices,* by Paul Fleischman, performed by John Bedford Lloyd and Anne Twomey, available from Harper & Row)

Copy of *Joyful Noise* for student reader (optional)

Materials

Student copies of *Joyful Noise*

Tape recorder and prerecorded version of "House Crickets" (optional)

1. Have the students listen as you play for them a reading of "House Crickets" that you and a colleague have recorded on audiotape in advance of the class. Alternatively, play the recording of the poem available on cassette tape from Harper & Row, publishers of *Joyful Noise*. Or, prior to class, carefully prepare to read the poem aloud with one of your students, you taking the left-hand part and the student the right-hand part.

Set the stage for your reading or tape playback by helping your students focus their attention on the poem. Ask them to imagine how it would feel not to have to worry about the weather of the different seasons of the year.

Play the prerecorded version of the poem or read the poem to the students. Read with appropriate expression to help the students apply their imaginations to the poem.

2. Distribute copies of *Joyful Noise* to the students and have them follow in their copies as you play for them once again the prerecorded version of "House Crickets" or as you reread the poem together with the student with whom you practiced.

Ask the students what they pictured in their minds as they listened to "House Crickets." Ask if they were able to imagine the way house crickets become aware of the change of seasons.

Materials

Student copies of *Joyful Noise*

Tape recorders for use by student pairs

Materials

Students' personal dictionaries

After the Reading

Materials

Writing paper; pens or pencils

3. Allow the students to read "House Crickets" again, silently. Then pair students and ask each pair to practice reading the poem, or selected portions of it, together. Have one reader take the left-hand part of the poem and the other the right-hand part, both speaking at the same time all lines printed on the same horizontal level.

Give pairs opportunities to record and play back their readings to help them achieve a smooth presentation of the poem. When they are ready, have them read the poem or selected portion to the class or to a small group within the class. Or they may play back a recording they have made of their reading.

Pair students who have difficulty with this oral presentation with students more skilled at it than they. Assist pairs as needed.

4. Have students add to their personal dictionaries any unfamiliar words they encounter in "House Crickets." Encourage them to seek from other students—reading partners, cooperative group members, and so on—suggestions about the meanings and pronunciations of the words. If you have distributed copies of the Glossary, encourage them to look up the meanings of the words and terms.

1. Poetry Idea: Change of Seasons. Recall with the students how house crickets know the seasons change: from the different types of food accidentally dropped on the floor by the humans who occupy the house in which the crickets dwell. Ask the students how they can tell that the seasons are changing. Suggest that such changes may be signaled not only by weather but also by human responses to weather, such as the types of clothes we wear, the activities in which we participate, the foods we eat, and so on.

Invite the students to write poems of their own about how they can tell the seasons are changing. Suggest they begin their poems "I know spring (or summer, fall, winter) is coming/When…," and use that refrain throughout their poems, as they describe as many indicators of seasonal change as they can.

Answer any questions the students may have about this poetry idea. Tell them they might write serious poems or humorous poems—or a combination of the two. If necessary, offer examples of the kinds of lines they might write. ("I know spring is coming/When water striders begin to skate on the surface of the pond/I know spring is coming/When I start thinking about playing baseball again.")

When you are confident the students understand the instructions, encourage them to begin writing. Circulate among them and offer assistance.

Encourage the students to share with one another their work in progress. Have those who complete their poems quickly work together with students who are having difficulty, or have them write an additional change of seasons poem.

When the students have completed their poems, invite them to read them aloud to the class. Respond enthusiastically and seek clarification when necessary. Post the students' poems in the classroom for all to read. Save the poems you have posted, as possible contributions to a book of student poetry to be compiled when the poetry teaching unit has been completed.

Materials

Activity Sheet 1 (one per student, pair, or cooperative group)

Printed resources about insects

Pens or pencils; drawing instruments

Sweeping nets (optional; see Activity Sheet 2)

Clear glass, wide-mouthed jars (optional)

10-power magnifying glass (optional)

Terrariums created of clear glass, wide-mouthed jars furnished with dirt and plants (optional)

2. What Do You Know About House Crickets? Ask how many students have ever seen a house cricket. Ask those who have to describe the settings in which they have seen house crickets. Ask: What does a house cricket look like? How does it move? What does it sound like?

Point out that, contrary to what their name suggests, house crickets generally live outdoors, often in garbage dumps. Tell them that house crickets are fond of warmth, however, and often enter houses in the fall, when the weather turns cold.

Distribute to the students copies of Activity Sheet 1. Provide them with or guide them to resources they may use to gather information about house crickets so they may complete the activity sheet. (See the Recommended Reading and Audiovisual Resources and Biological Supply Houses lists at the end of the literature teaching guide. Encyclopedias and books on general biology or the life sciences may also provide information to help students complete the activity sheet.)

In addition, if time of year and location are appropriate, encourage the students to gather as much information about house crickets as they can simply by observing the insects in their natural habitats. Tell them that with care and quick reflexes they may be able to capture house crickets in fine mesh sweeping nets (see Activity Sheet 2) and transfer them to clear glass, wide-mouthed jars with hole-punched lids so they can observe the insects closely.

Remind the students that they might also find a magnifying glass helpful in observing the details of the house cricket's structure and coloring. Finally, tell your students to be sure to return the house crickets to their natural outdoor habitat when their observations have been completed.

As an adjunct or alternative to observations individual students conduct of house crickets in their natural habitats, arrange for students to conduct observations in the classroom setting. Have one or more students capture house crickets, in the manner just described, and bring them to the classroom. Or check to see whether live specimens are available from one of the biological supply houses listed at the end of this teaching guide. Place the crickets in terrariums created by adding soil and plants to large, wide-mouthed jars placed on their sides. Tell them to make sure the jar lids have air holes punched in them. Encourage the students to observe and record the physical characteristics of the house crickets, their eating habits, and so on. Encourage them to use the house crickets as models for illustrations they make on their activity sheets.

Allow students to conduct their research and field observations individually, with partners, or in small groups of three or four students. Remind them that each member of a pair or cooperative group should be prepared to demonstrate the tasks each performed and that all students should be able to explain any of the information provided on the completed activity sheet.

When the students have completed their activity sheets, invite them to report to their classmates the information they have gathered. If information provided by students differs, have them cite their sources of information—printed materials, audiovisual resources, and field observations—and try to determine why there are differences among the reports. Finally, have the individual students, pairs, or cooperative groups keep the activity sheets they have prepared on house crickets to combine in a class publication with similar activity sheets on the other insects featured in the poems of *Joyful Noise*.

FOR THE TEACHER

Insect Name: *House Cricket*

Phylum: *Arthropoda*

Class: *Insecta*

Order: *Orthoptera*

Family: *Gryllidae*

General Physical Characteristics: *House crickets are difficult to distinguish from field crickets. They are light brown or shiny black in color. Their antennae are longer than their bodies. They have two rather long appendages, called* cerci, *extending from the end of their abdomen. These are believed to be sensory in function.*

Adult house crickets range from 6/10 to 9/10 of an inch in adult body length. Like grasshoppers, the femora of their hind legs are enlarged, giving them exceptional jumping abilities.

Typical Behavior: *The most distinctive behavior of house crickets is their intermittent, shrill chirping. Their call, which is produced by males of the species, is part of courtship. Like katydids, crickets produce their call by rubbing together roughened files at the base of their forewings. The rate of their chirping seems to depend on the temperature. In general, it speeds up when it is warmer and slows down when it is colder. They also appear to be more active at night than during the day.*

House crickets feed on plants outdoors and sometimes damage woolens and carpets indoors.

Habitat: *House crickets are found throughout North America. They generally live outdoors, often in or near garbage dumps. Fond of the warmth, they enter houses and bakeries when the weather turns cold.*

Life Cycle: *Female house crickets lay their eggs singly on the ground during summer. The eggs overwinter in the soil and hatch the following spring or summer.*

Materials

Computers and database or hypermedia software

As an alternative to completing the written portions of the activity sheet, if computers and appropriate database or hypermedia software are available, encourage the students to add to their insect databases or hypermedia stacks or folders. (A listing of appropriate database fields is provided in descriptions of this activity for use with poems that appear earlier in Fleischman's collection.)

Materials

Student copies of *Joyful Noise*

Two pots of water for boiling, one large and one small

Two thermometers for measuring boiling water

Two burners able to be set at equal levels of heat

3. Temperature Conversions. Refer the students to the lines of "House Crickets" in which the narrator crickets point out that they "live in a world of fixed Fahrenheit." Ask the students what that statement means. Ask what it would be like to live in an environment in which they did not have to be concerned about the weather, in which temperatures were always constant.

Use this opportunity to review with students the nature of temperature and the different ways of measuring it. Write the word *temperature* on the chalkboard. Ask the students what the term means. Perform the following demonstration to help them distinguish between *temperature* and *heat.*

Fill two pots, one large and one small, with water. Place the pots on burners, each at the same setting. Place a thermometer in each pot. Have the students observe how long it takes each pot to come to a boiling point. They will draw the obvious conclusion that the water in the smaller pot requires less heat to reach boiling temperature than the water in the larger pot.

Ask the students to explain what happens to a substance as it becomes hotter. Tell them that all substances—solids, liquids, and gases—are made up of basic particles of matter called *atoms* and *molecules,* which are always moving randomly about. The energy of this motion is called *kinetic energy.* The faster the particles of a substance move, the greater the substance's kinetic energy.

Explain that when a substance is heated, its atoms and molecules move faster. The *heat* of a substance is the *total* kinetic energy of the random motion of the substances's atoms and molecules. Accordingly, the greater the number of particles in a substance, the more heat energy it contains.

Explain that the larger of the two pots of boiling water contains more heat energy than the smaller pot because it has a greater number of atoms and molecules. Point out that, nevertheless, the temperature of the water in each pot is the same—100° C. That is because the temperature of a substance is the *average* kinetic energy of the particles that make up the substance. Thus, two substances can have the same temperature, but different amounts of heat energy.

Tell the students that air temperature actually is a measure of the average speed of the molecules in the air. For example, on a day when the temperature measures 30°C, the average speed of the molecules in the air is about 440 m/s. On a day when the temperature measures –20°C, however, the average speed of the molecules is only about 400 m/s.

Ask the students how temperature generally is measured. Explain that the *instrument* commonly used to measure temperature is the *thermometer.* Explain further that there are three different scales used to measure temperature:

- the absolute temperature scale, in which the standard unit is the Kelvin (K); this is the standard measuring system used by scientists all over the world.

- the centigrade scale, in which the standard unit is the Celsius (C) degree.

- the Fahrenheit scale, in which the standard unit is the Fahrenheit (F) degree.

The Kelvin unit is named after the Irish-born physicist William Thompson, the first Baron Kelvin (1824–1907), who did pioneering work on the mechanical properties of heat. In the absolute temperature scale, water freezes at 273 K and boils at 373K. The Celsius degree is named after Swedish physicist Anders Celsius (1701–1744), who developed a scale in which the freezing point of water is designated as 0° and the boiling point as 100°. Celsius named his scale *centigrade* because it had 100 equal intervals between the two points.

Explain to the students how to convert from Kelvin to Celsius: Subtract 273 from the temperature in Kelvin. Emphasize that the Celsius scale and the related absolute temperature scale are used in most parts of the world today for measuring temperature and temperature changes.

Finally, explain that the Fahrenheit scale is named after German physicist G. D. Fahrenheit (1686–1736), who developed a thermometer in which mercury that had been sealed inside a bulb attached to a tube expanded and contracted as the ambient temperature rose and fell. Fahrenheit attached a scale to the side of the tube, according to which the temperature could be read. In the Fahrenheit scale, which is used in the United States, particularly in popular weather reports, water freezes at 32°F and boils at 212°F.

Explain to the students how to convert from Fahrenheit to Celsius: Subtract 32 from the Fahrenheit temperature and multiply the remainder by 5/9. (To convert Celsius to Fahrenheit, reverse the procedure: Add 32 to the Celsius temperature and multiply the sum by 9/5.)

Give the students opportunities to convert temperatures among the three scales commonly used. Suggest, for example, that the house crickets' fixed Fahrenheit is a comfortable 68°. Ask the students to convert that temperature to the Celsius and absolute temperature scales. Select other temperatures for conversion: the current day's temperature, average healthy body temperature, and so on.

Materials

Student copies of *Joyful Noise*

Writing paper; pens or pencils

Dictionaries, thesauruses

4. Sounds Like... Ask the students how they would write the sound that a dog (or horse, bird, etc.) makes. Invite volunteer students to come to the chalkboard and offer their suggestions.

Select from among their suggestions the actual words some students have written (*bark, neigh, peep,* etc.) Explain that there are a number of words in English that seem to sound like the object or event they describe. Ask a student to say the word *bark* loudly and sharply; point out that the sound is similar to that a dog would make. Follow a similar procedure with other words listed.

If you think it useful, tell the students that words that imitate the natural sound of an object or event are called *onomatopoeia*.

Ask the students what word poet Paul Fleischman uses in "House Crickets" to indicate the sound crickets make. *(crick-et)* Ask whether they think his choice a good one.

Ask the students to examine other poems in *Joyful Noise* to see if the poet uses other such words. (In "Cicadas" Fleischman describes the insects "humming...buzzing...whirring...whining.")

Group the students in fours and have them develop lists that include as many words as possible that imitate the natural sounds of objects or events. Provide them with dictionaries and thesauruses. Their lists might include such words as *howl, croak, moan, moo, whinny, knock, puff, cuckoo, crackle, whiz, whoosh, zoom, click*. Alternatively, have students search through your classroom collection of books—particularly books of folk tales and poetry—to find examples of such words.

When the groups have completed their task, have a reporter from each group share the group's list with the class. Invite class members to judge whether the words listed are appropriate. When all the groups have reported their selections, have each student choose his or her favorite selection and describe, orally or in writing, why he or she selected the particular word.

CHRYSALIS DIARY

Before the Reading

Prepare your students to read Paul Fleischman's poem "Chrysalis Diary" by using one or both of the following suggestions:

1. Write the word *change* in large letters on the chalkboard. Brainstorm with the students to develop a list of changes they have experienced, internally and externally, during the last year. Cluster their suggestions around the word *change,* or have a volunteer student do so.

Ask the students to indicate which of the changes they initiated, which were initiated by others, and which simply occurred as part of human growth. Ask which changes they think are most likely to have the greatest effect on them.

Tell the students they are about to listen to and read a poem in which Paul Fleischman describes a profound change that an insect undergoes. Encourage them to listen carefully to determine what kind of insect the poet describes and what sort of effect the change will have on the insect's future.

2. Ask if any students have ever kept diaries or if they know of anyone famous who has done so. (Ask, for example, if they are familiar with the diary written by Anne Frank, in which the young Jewish woman recorded her intimate thoughts about her own personal growth as well as about the trial her family underwent as they hid from Nazi soldiers in World War II Amsterdam. Display a copy of the diary, if possible.) Ask why a person might keep a diary. Suggest that keeping a diary can be a way of recording, and thus clarifying, one's inmost thoughts and feelings for an audience of one.

Tell the students they are about to listen to and read a poem written in the form of a diary. Encourage them listen carefully to discover the author of the diary and the sort of revelations it contains.

Materials

Copy of Anne Frank's diary or other famous diary for display

During the Reading

Materials

Teacher copy of *Joyful Noise*

Tape recorder and prerecorded version of "Chrysalis Diary" (optional; a cassette tape, *Joyful Noise and I Am Phoenix, Poems for Two Voices,* by Paul Fleischman, performed by John Bedford Lloyd and Anne Twomey, available from Harper & Row)

Copy of *Joyful Noise* for student reader (optional)

1. Have the students listen as you play for them a reading of "Chrysalis Diary" that you and a colleague have recorded on audiotape in advance of the class. Alternatively, play the recording of the poem available on cassette tape from Harper & Row, publishers of *Joyful Noise.* Or, prior to class, carefully prepare to read the poem aloud along with one of your students, you taking the left-hand part and the student the right-hand part.

Set the stage for your reading or tape playback by helping your students focus their attention on the poem. Ask them to imagine what it might feel like to experience something unknown or fearful without having anyone to rely on or talk with.

Play the prerecorded version of the poem or read the poem to the students. Read with appropriate expression to help the students apply their imaginations to the poem. Help them visualize the gradual changes that the caterpillar undergoes within its cocoon while dramatic changes in season take place outside.

Materials

Student copies of *Joyful Noise*

Tape recorder and prerecorded version of "Chrysalis Diary" (optional)

Materials

Student copies of *Joyful Noise*

Tape recorders for use by student pairs

Materials

Students' personal dictionaries

After the Reading

Materials

Writing paper; pens or pencils

2. Distribute copies of *Joyful Noise* to the students and have them follow in their copies as you play for them once again the prerecorded version of "Chrysalis Diary" or as you reread the poem together with the student with whom you practiced.

Ask the students what they pictured in their minds as they listened to "Chrysalis Diary." Ask if they were able to imagine the unsettling silence the caterpillar experienced within its cocoon, the caterpillar's sense of wonder at winter's world of white, its uncertainty about what was taking place within its body. Ask what moods the poem evokes in them.

3. Allow the students to read "Chrysalis Diary" again, silently. Then pair students and ask each pair to practice reading the poem, or selected portions of it, together. Have one reader take the left-hand part of the poem and the other the right-hand part. Tell both readers to read from top to bottom, both speaking at the same time all lines printed on the same horizontal level.

Give pairs opportunities to record and play back their readings to help them achieve a smooth presentation of the poem. When they are ready, have them read the poem or selected portion to the class or to a small group within the class. Or they may play back a recording they have made of their reading.

Pair students who have difficulty with this oral presentation with more skilled students. Assist pairs as needed.

4. Have students add to their personal dictionaries any unfamiliar words they encounter in "Chrysalis Diary." Encourage them to seek from other students—reading partners, cooperative group members, and so on—suggestions about the meanings and pronunciations of the words. If you have distributed copies of the Glossary, encourage them to look up the meanings of the words and terms.

1. Poetry Idea: A Diary Poem. Ask the students what a diary is (or recall your discussion of diaries, if you talked about them before the reading). Suggest that diaries offer individuals opportunities to write down, often for themselves alone, their inmost thoughts and feelings and in that way to come to understand themselves better. Ask how what the butterfly caterpillar wrote may be considered material appropriate for a diary.

Invite the students to write diary poems of their own, inspired by Paul Fleischman's "Chrysalis Diary." Suggest that they write their diary poems individually, during the week, beginning with today. Suggest they begin each diary entry with the date, as Fleischman did, and then describe how they felt about at least one thing that happened to them on that day that was important, humorous, unsettling, astounding, stimulating, and so on.

Answer any questions the students may have about this poetry idea. Tell them they might write serious poems or humorous poems—or a combination of the two. If necessary, offer examples of the kinds of lines they might write ("May 4:/I felt the warmth of spring/and I wanted to shout 'Hooray!/I could hardly wait/for class to end/so I could get outside with my friends.")

When you are sure the students understand the instructions, encourage them to begin writing. Circulate among them and offer assistance.

Encourage the students to share with one another their initial diary entries as they write them. Have those who quickly complete their first entries work together with students who are having difficulty getting started.

When the week-long period has been completed, invite the students to read their diary poems aloud to the class. Respond with enthusiasm, seeking clarification when necessary. Post the students' poems in the classroom for all to read. Save the poems you have posted, as possible contributions to a book of student poetry to be compiled when the poetry teaching unit has been completed.

2. What Do You Know About Butterflies? Ask how many students have ever seen a butterfly. Ask those who have to describe the time of year and the settings in which they have seen butterflies. Ask: What did the butterflies you saw look like? What colors were they? Have you seen any butterfly caterpillars? What did they look like?

Point out that butterflies are day fliers and are often seen around flowers whose nectar they seek as food.

Distribute to the students copies of Activity Sheet 1. Provide them with or guide them to resources they may use to gather information about butterflies so they may complete the activity sheet. Tell them to try to find a family or species of butterfly that changes form from caterpillar to adult butterfly in the manner and at the time of year described by Paul Fleischman. (See the Recommended Reading and Audiovisual Resources and Biological Supply Houses lists at the end of the literature teaching guide. Encyclopedias and books on general biology or the life sciences may also provide information to help students complete the activity sheet.)

In addition, if time of year and location are appropriate, encourage the students to gather as much information about butterflies as they can simply by observing the insects in their natural habitats. Tell them that with care and quick reflexes they may be able to capture butterflies in fine mesh sweeping nets (see Activity Sheet 2) and transfer them to clear glass, wide-mouthed jars with hole-punched lids so they can observe the insects closely. Tell them that for this assignment, they may capture any species of butterfly, not just those, like mourning cloaks, that pupate in the manner described in the poem.

Remind the students that they might also find a magnifying glass helpful in observing the details of the butterfly's structure and coloring. Finally, tell your students to be sure to return the butterflies to their natural habitat when their observations have been completed.

As an adjunct or alternative to observations individual students conduct of butterflies in their natural habitats, arrange for students to conduct observations in the classroom setting. Have one or more students capture butterflies in the manner just described, and bring them to the classroom. Or check to see whether live specimens are available from one of the biological supply houses listed at the end of the teaching guide. Place the butterflies in terrariums created by adding soil and plants to large, wide-mouthed jars placed on their sides. (Tell them to make sure the jar lids have air holes punched in them.) Provide sugar (or honey) in water as food. Encourage the students to observe and record the physical characteristics of the butterflies, their eating habits, and so on. Encourage them to use the butterflies as models for illustrations they make on their activity sheets.

Materials

Activity Sheet 1 (one per student, pair, or cooperative group)

Printed resources about insects

Pens or pencils; drawing instruments

Sweeping nets (optional; see Activity Sheet 2)

Clear glass, wide-mouthed jars (optional)

10-power magnifying glass (optional)

Terrariums created of clear glass, wide-mouthed jars furnished with dirt, plants and sugar (or honey) mixed in water

Allow students to conduct their research and field observations individually, with partners, or in small groups of three or four students. Remind them that each member of a pair or cooperative group should be prepared to demonstrate the tasks each performed and that all students should be able to explain any of the information provided on the completed activity sheet.

When the students have completed their activity sheets, invite them to report to their classmates the information they have gathered. If information provided by students differs, have them cite their sources of information—printed materials, audiovisual resources, and field observations—and try to determine why there are differences among the reports. Finally, have the individual students, pairs, or cooperative groups keep the activity sheets they have prepared on butterflies to combine in a class publication with similar activity sheets on the other insects featured in the poems of *Joyful Noise*.

FOR THE TEACHER

Insect Name: *Butterfly*

Phylum: *Arthropoda*

Class: *Insecta*

Order: *Lepidoptera*

Family: *There are several families of butterflies, including Nymphalidae, Papilionidae, Hesperidae, and Riodinidae. Mourning cloak butterflies, which may pupate in the manner and at the time of year described in "Chrysalis Diary," are members of the family Nymphalidae.*

General Physical Characteristics: *The name* Lepidoptera *means "scaly-wings," indicating the tiny, flat scales that cover the wings, legs, and bodies of butterflies and moths alike, much as shingles cover the roofs of buildings. The scales, which come off when members of this order struggle to free themselves—for example, from spider webs—serve as a protective adaptation.*

The scales come in many shapes, patterns, and colors, helping to identify particular species of butterflies and moths and giving them their distinctive beauty.

It is difficult to distinguish butterflies and moths. The antennae of butterflies end in a club, whereas the antennae of most moths are tapered or feathery. Most butterflies rest with their wings held vertical, with the upper sides over the back, whereas most moths rest with the wings flat over the back. Butterflies have no attachment between the wings, which overlap; in most moths the wings are attached to each other by one or more bristles at the base of the hindwing. Most butterflies are diurnal—they are day fliers—whereas most moths are nocturnal in habit.

The mourning cloak butterfly, which pupates in the manner described in "Chrysalis Diary," is also called the "spiny elm caterpillar." Its velvety, purplish brown wings have a wide yellow border or margin and a submarginal row of blue spots. Its wing spread ranges from 2 3/4 to 3 1/4

129

inches. It belongs to the family Nymphalidae, the members of which are commonly called "brush-footed butterflies," indicating their hairy and brushlike front legs, which are greatly reduced in size in comparison with their other two pairs of legs.

Typical Behavior: *Mourning cloak butterflies are strong fliers and are generally most active at midday.*

Habitat: *Mourning cloak butterflies are found near willow, poplar, alder, and elm trees throughout Canada and the United States.*

Life Cycle: *Butterflies, including mourning cloak butterflies, have four principal life stages: the egg, the caterpillar or larva, the chrysalis or pupa, and the adult. After an elaborate courtship, males and females mate. Females lay their eggs on or near a suitable food plant for the caterpillars and in a site with suitable temperature and humidity and adequate protection. Caterpillars spend their time feeding. They usually undergo four molts, the last of which reveals the pupa or chrysalis. The chrysalis is the cocoon in which the caterpillar's tissues are broken down and used to feed cells that had remained dormant but that will become the adult butterfly. In the last days of summer, the mourning cloak caterpillar attaches itself to a twig by means of a silken button and hangs upside down. In early spring the adult butterfly emerges.*

Materials

Computers and database or hypermedia software

Materials

Computers and database or hypermedia software

Student-created databases of insects

As an alternative to completing the written portions of the activity sheet, if computers and appropriate database or hypermedia software are available, encourage the students to add to their insect databases or hypermedia stacks or folders. (A listing of appropriate database fields is provided in descriptions of this activity for use with poems that appear earlier in Fleischman's collection.)

3. Organizing and Retrieving Information. Invite the students who have created databases or hypermedia stacks or folders of information about the insects described in Paul Fleischman's poems to share their creations with their classmates. Give each student an opportunity to explain to the whole class or to a smaller group within the class how the software they used allows information to be organized and retrieved. Have them demonstrate, for example, how the software might allow them to retrieve information about all the insects that belong to a particular order, such as Lepidoptera, or to arrange the insects in order by specific characteristics, such as adult body length or length of time required for growth to maturity.

Encourage students to suggest ways in which their databases or hypermedia stacks or folders about insects might be put to use. Elicit from them other areas of study in which the creation of databases, stacks, or folders might help them learn. Try to make computers and appropriate software available to them for use in conjunction with other coursework.

Materials

Student-created poems inspired by *Joyful Noise*

Copies of Activity Sheet 1 prepared by individuals, pairs, or cooperative groups

Printouts of insect databases or hypermedia stacks or folders compiled by students

Computers; appropriate word processing, graphics, database, hypermedia, and page layout software; printer

Paper, pens and pencils, and materials with which students can create illustrations for their books

Staplers to bind books

4. Class Books. Give the students opportunities, as a whole class or in smaller groups, to create a book or books that feature the poems they have composed or the insect information sheets they compiled individually, with partners, or with small groups (their copies of Activity Sheet 1 for each of the poems in *Joyful Noise* or printouts of their individual database files or hypermedia stacks or folders for each insect). If time permits, have students create both types of books. Encourage the students to create the most attractive, appealing books they can.

Here are the tasks the book publishers need to perform:

- Select the student-created materials that will be included in the book. Each student might select his or her best poem or each student, pair, or cooperative group might choose its best compilation of information about a specific insect. Or the class or cooperative group publishing the book might choose favorites from among all the contributions available. A composition or compilation by each student should be included in the completed book.

- Determine how the book will be laid out, that is, what will appear on which page, what the sequence of elements will be, what design elements will be added to the text to make the book appealing, and so forth. Encourage the students to examine *Joyful Noise* carefully for ideas about how a book may be attractively designed. Tell the students to pay attention not only to placement of text and use of illustrations but also to use of white space and different typefaces and sizes.

- Assign students specific tasks to perform, or have the students volunteer for the tasks. Tasks include *word processing,* if computers and appropriate software are available (if they are not available, have the students prepare by hand copies of their contributions that they will be proud to have included in the book); *illustration,* for the body of the book and for the cover, which may be done by hand or generated on computer, if computers and graphics software are available; *page layout,* which also may be done by hand or on computer; *page collation and bookbinding.* Each student should participate, performing at least one of the book publishing tasks.

Give the students sufficient time to complete their publication. Provide assistance as needed. Encourage the students to choose a title for their book.

When the book or books have been completed, display them in the classroom. If possible, display them in the school library and make them available for other students and teachers to read.

5. Word Games. Group the students in fives or sixes. Have each student bring his or her personal dictionary.

Materials

Students' personal dictionaries

- Have each group arrange itself in a circle. Then have one student read a definition from his or her personal dictionary to the student on his or her left. If that student is able to name the word that matches the definition, then he or she selects a definition to be read to the next person, and so on. If a student is unable to name the word that matches a particular definition, the opportunity to name the word moves down the line to the next person. Continue as long as the game retains the students' interest or until all the definitions in the students' dictionaries have been used.

- Select a relatively lengthy word from the Glossary or have students suggest such words from their personal dictionaries. Write the word on the chalkboard. Give each student five minutes to write down as many words as he or she can using only the letters contained in the starter word. Tell them the following rules apply:

Words must be at least four letters in length.

Proper nouns may not be used.

Foreign words, abbreviations, and plurals may not be used.

Both the present and the past tense of the same verb may not be used.

A letter may be used in a listed word no more than the number of times it is found in the starter word.

All disputes will be resolved by reference to a dictionary.

Some of the words that may be built from the word *perseverance*, for example, are the following:

severe	serve	race
sever	care	near
scare	pare	presence
preserve	never	reverse
reserve	even	ever
seen	pace	pane
peer	reap	pear
seer	rear	prance
rave	vane	never
cane	span	seance
rare	creep	revere

When 5 minutes are up, give the students an additional 5 to 10 minutes to compare their individual lists with those of other group members. Have the groups compile master lists, eliminating duplicates and adding new words suggested by the entries on each individual list. Finally, have the groups report the entries on their lists. Determine which group developed the lengthiest list, the most ingenious list, the list with the greatest number of lengthy words, the list with the most amusing words, and so on.

- Have each group compose a short story using as many words from its members' personal dictionaries as possible. Set a time limit of 5 to 10 minutes. When the time is up, have the groups read their stories aloud. Determine which group used the most personal dictionary words, which composed the cleverest story, which included the best single sentence, and so on.

Materials

Paper and pencil for each student
Dictionaries

Recommended Reading About Insects

Reference Books

Blough, Glenn O. *Discovering Insects.* New York: McGraw-Hill, 1967.

Borror, D. J., D. M. DeLong, and C. A. Triplehorn. *An Introduction to the Study of Insects.* 6th ed. SCP: Philadelphia, 1989.

Butler, Colin G. *The World of the Honeybee.* London: Collins, 1974.

Klots, Alexander B., and Elsie B. Klots. *Living Insects of the World.* Garden City, NY: Doubleday, 1967.

_____. *1001 Questions Answered About Insects.* New York: Dover Publications, 1977.

O'Toole, Christopher, ed. *The Encyclopedia of Insects.* New York: Facts on File, 1986.

Pyle, Robert Michael. *The Audubon Society's Handbook for Butterfly Watchers.* New York: Charles Scribner's Sons, 1984.

Stokes, Donald. *A Guide to Observing Insect Lives.* Boston: Little, Brown, 1983.

Swan, Lester A., and Charles S. Papp. *Common Insects of North America.* New York: Harper & Row, 1972.

Field Guides

Arnett, R. H., Jr., and R. L. Jaques, Jr. *Simon and Schuster's Guide to Insects.* New York: Simon and Schuster, 1981.

Borror, Donald J., and Richard E. White. *A Field Guide to the Insects of America North of Mexico.* Boston: Houghton Mifflin, 1970.

Familiar Insects and Spiders: An Audubon Society Pocket Guide. New York: Knopf, 1988.

Milne, L., and M. Milne. *The Audubon Society's Field Guide to North American Insects and Spiders.* New York: Knopf, 1980.

Powell, Jerry A., and Charles L. Hogue. *California Insects.* Berkeley, CA: University of California Press, 1979.

Pyle, Robert Michael. *The Audubon Society's Field Guide to North American Butterflies.* New York: Knopf, 1981.

Specifically for Children

Conklin, Gladys. *The Bug Book Club: A Handbook for Young Bug Collectors.* New York: Holiday House, 1966.

Goor, Ron, and Nancy Goor. *Insect Metamorphosis: From Egg to Adult.* New York: Atheneum, 1990.

Hogner, Dorothy Childs. *Moths.* New York: Crowell, 1964.

Mound, Lawrence. *Insect.* New York: Knopf, 1990.

Tee-Van, Helen Damrosch. *Insects Are Where You Find Them: A Simple Introduction to the Most Common American Insects.* New York: Knopf, 1963.

Also:

Dunn, Gary A. *Buggy Books: A Guide to Juvenile and Popular Books on Insects and Their Relatives.* Lansing, MI: Young Entomologists Society, 1990. A guide to 736 nonfiction spider and insect books published since 1900 for young people and the general public. Includes annotated bibliographical listings and an age-appropriateness index by title.

Audiovisual Resources and Biological Supply Houses

Audiovisual Resources

Arthropods: An Introduction to Insects and Their Relatives. Carolina Biological Supply Co., 2700 York Rd., Burlington, NC 28215. (57 slides, teacher guide, puzzles, worksheets)

Discovering Insects: Orders. Screenscope, Inc., Suite 204, 3600 M. St., NW, Washington, D. C. 20007. (film; 12 min.; teacher guide)

Insect Anatomy Up Close. Educational Images, Ltd., P.O. Box 367, Lyons Falls, NY 13368. (slide set)

Insects: How They Help Us. National Geographic Society Educational Services, 17th & M Streets NW, Washington, D.C. 20036. (filmstrip, 15 min.; cassette and guides)

Insects—Little Giants of the Earth. Coronet/MTI, 108 Wilmot Rd., Deerfield, IL 60015. (Laserdisc with teacher guides; requires Apple Macintosh™)

Insect Metapmorphosis Up Close. Educational Images, Inc. (See address above; slide set.)

Insects. Oxford Scientific Films. Available from Carolina Biological Supply Co. (See address above; 50 slides covering 19 insect orders.)

Life Cycle of the Honeybee. Biosciences Series, National Geographic Society Educational Services, 17th & M Streets NW, Washington, D. C. 20036. (film with teacher guide)

Life on Earth, Vol. 2, "The Swarming Hordes," Films, Inc., Learning Materials Division, 50 Ridge Ave. Extension, Cambridge, MA 02140.(filmstrip, with cassette and teacher guide)

The World of Insects. National Geographic Society Educational Services, 17th & M Streets NW, Washington, D. C. 20036. (20-minute color video)

Biological Supply Houses

The Biology Store, P. O. Box 2691, Escondido, CA 92033; (619) 745-1445; toll-free in California and Nevada: 1-800-654-0792; FAX (619) 489-2268.

Carolina Biolgical Supply Co., 2700 York Rd., Burlington, NC 27215; (910) 584-0381; toll-free 1-800-334-5551; or P.O. Box 187, Gladstone OR 97027; (503) 656-1641; toll-free 1-800-547-1733.

Insect Lore Products, P.O. Box 1535, Shafter, CA 93263; customer service: (805) 746-6047; orders only 1-800-LIVE-BUG; FAX: (805) 746-0334.

Wards Natural Science Establishment, Inc., 5100 West Henrietta Rd., Rochester, NY 14692; (716) 359-2502; toll-free 1-800-962-2660.

Miscellaneous

Young Entomologists' Society, Inc., 1915 Peggy Place, Lansing, MI 48910-2553; (517) 887-0499. Order a catalog for a list of books, educational materials, and kits available.

Entomological Society of America, 4603 Calvert Rd., College Park, MD 20740; (301)731-4535. A source of information for the profession.

Joyful Noise: Poems for Two Voices
A Glossary

attendant   one who waits on another, 29

backtrack   to retrace one's course, 3

balderdash   nonsense, 6

boisterous   loud, noisy, unrestrained, 28

bough   branch of a tree, especially a large or main branch, 42

bound   headed for; going toward, 22

bound   to leap forward or upward; to spring or vault, 4

burrow   hole or tunnel dug in the ground for habitation or shelter, 25

calligrapher   one who produces fine or elegant handwriting, 13

cataclysm   violent and sudden change, 41

cherish   to hold dear; to treat with affection and tenderness; to care for, 25 and 42

Christie, Agatha.   1891–1976. English mystery novelist and playwright, 15

chrysalis   stage in the development of an insect, especially of a moth or butterfly, following the larval stage and preceding the adult form; during this inactive stage the developing insect is enclosed in a firm case or cocoon, 39

cockswain   [also *coxswain*] A person who steers a boat or racing shell and has charge of its crew, 21

compass   device for determining directions by means of a magnetic needle free to pivot until pointing to the magnetic north, 19

Conan Doyle   Sir Arthur Conan Doyle, 1859–1930. British novelist and detective story writer. Conan Doyle, also a physician, is especially well known for his stories about Sherlock Holmes, 17

contrasting   showing or having differences or dissimilarities, 16

discern   to detect, discover, perceive; to come to know, 24

drone   to make a sustained, deep humming sound or buzz, 27

edition   printing; one of the whole number of copies of a text published at one time, 15

emerge   to come into existence, 8

Fahrenheit   of or relating to a temperature scale that registers the freezing point at 32 degrees above zero and the boiling point at 212 degrees above zero under standard atmospheric pressure, 38

fervent   showing great feeling or warmth, 27

film   thin covering or coating, 7

frantic   frenzied, wild; filled with wild excitement, 9

gladiator   professional combatant, 35

gyrate   to wind or revolve around a center or axis; to circle or spiral, 33

Horace   65–8 B.C.E. Roman poet and satirist, 17

jubilant   joyful, rejoicing, 27

kiln   oven or furnace used for hardening, burning or drying substances, 26

larva   immature, wingless, often wormlike form of a newly hatched insect before it undergoes the transformation known as *metamorphosis* whereby it becomes an adult, 30

miser   one who deprives himself or herself of all but the barest necessities in order to hoard wealth. Here used as a verb to mean *to collect and store*, 42

multitudes   great, indefinite number, 41

nectar   sweet liquid secreted by flowers of various plants which serves as the chief raw material for making honey, 18 and 30

parchment   skin of a sheep or a goat, prepared for writing on; paper prepared to resemble this material, 11

particle   very small part or bit, 9

perseverance steadfastness; singleness of purpose; determination, 24

plight trouble, dilemma; a condition of difficulty, 18

ponder to consider carefully, 42

prudent careful, cautious; exercising good judgment, 7

quince many-seeded, applelike fruit of a tree of the same name, which is native to western Asia. The fruit is used for making preserves, marmalade and jelly, 37

racing shell long, narrow, light racing boat propelled by one or more oarsmen, 22

replica copy or close reproduction, 25

reside to dwell, lodge, or live in a place for an extended period of time, 17

Roget's Thesaurus treasury of words originally compiled by Peter Mark Roget (1779–1869). It includes words listed and classified according to categories such as synonyms and antonyms, 17

Schiller Johann Christoph Friedrich von Schiller, 1759–1805. German poet and dramatist, 15

Scott Sir Walter Scott, 1771–1832. Scottish poet and novelist, 15

serpentine resembling a serpent in movement; winding, sinuous, twisting, 33

Shakespeare. William Shakespeare, 1564–1616. English dramatist and poet, 17

Spillane. Frank Morrison Spillane, 1918– . American detective story writer, known for a violent form of hard-boiled fiction and a blunt narrative style. Spillane's chief character is detective Mike Hammer and among his best known works are *I, the Jury* (1947) and *Kiss Me Deadly* (1952), 17

squander to waste; to spend extravagantly or wastefully, 9

thunderhead rounded upper portion of a thundercloud, often taken as a sign of an impending thunderstorm, 26

tortuous marked by repeated bends, twists or turns; winding, 33

trice brief period of time; an instant; a moment, 19

trifling insignificant; of small importance, 8

unionize to organize into a labor union or alliance of workers seeking to protect their interests in such matters as wages and working conditions, 31

vault to jump or leap over, 4

Insect Name:	
Phylum:	**Class:**
Order:	**Family:**

General Physical Characteristics (What does the insect look like?)

Typical Behavior (What does this insect do that identifies it?)

Habitat (In what type of area does this insect live?)

Life Cycle (How does this insect develop? How long does it live?)

Illustration (Draw or paste a picture of the insect here.)

Making a Sweeping Net

Sweeping nets are useful for capturing insects that live in grass and shrubbery. The nets are easy to make. You will need the following materials:

- A piece of wire about 36" long, sufficient when joined end-to-end to make a circle or hoop 12–16" in diameter (a wire coat hanger may be used)

- A broom handle or wooden rod about 5/8" thick and 3' long

- Nylon, muslin, or light canvas about 2 1/2 x 3'

- A roll of strong tape or a clamp

- Heavy thread

1. Use a backsaw or a file to cut grooves about 4" long on each side of one end of the handle. Make the grooves big enough to hold the legs of the wire.

2. Form the wire into a circle or hoop with a 4" leg at each end.

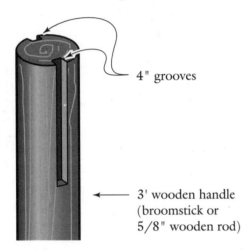

4" grooves

3' wooden handle (broomstick or 5/8" wooden rod)

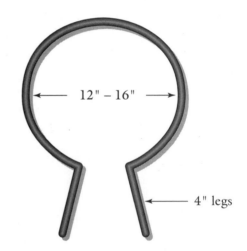

12" – 16"

4" legs

3. Force the legs of the wire into the grooves and tape or clamp them tightly.

4. Tape netting to hoop, or sew it on with heavy thread.

tape tightly wrapped around handle (or clamp tightened around handle

Making a Two-Handled Seine

Seines are useful for capturing water insects, such as water striders, water boatmen, and whirligig beetles in shallow water along stream, river, and lake edges. Two-handed seines are easy to make. You will need the following materials:

- Two broom handles or wooden rods about 3' long

- One piece of fine mesh wire screen or cloth netting 2 x 3'

- Lead sinkers

- One box of wire staples or large-headed tacks

1. Hem or reinforce the 2' sides of the screen or netting. Sew small lead sinkers into one edge, which will become the bottom edge of the netting when the seine is open.

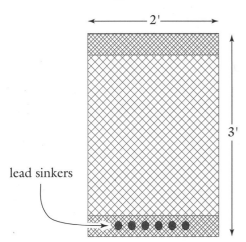

2. Wrap the 3' sides of the screen or netting tightly around the two handles or rods at least one and a half times.

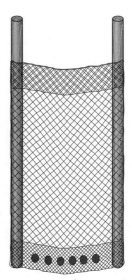

3. Tack the screen or netting to the rods, spacing the staples or tacks about 1" apart.

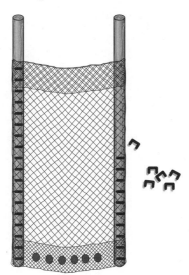

4. Remove your shoes and socks and wade from deeper water in toward the shore with the seine open, held on or near the bottom of the water.

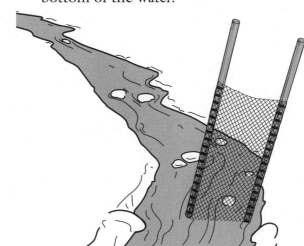

139

Name _____

Date _____

Pleasing Sounds

Poets and other writers sometimes try to please our listening ears by repeating the same sound at the beginning of two or more words that follow each other or are close to each other. Poet Paul Fleischman does so in his poem "Fireflies" and in other poems in *Joyful Noise*.

On the lines below, write all the examples of such pleasing sounds that you can find in "Fireflies" and in other Paul Fleischman poems you have read. Next to each example write the page number on which the example is found.

_____

_____

_____

_____

_____

Here are some other examples of such pleasing sounds:

■ The <u>w</u>ind <u>w</u>andered in and out of the canyons.

■ <u>Pl</u>ump <u>p</u>umpkins were <u>p</u>ropped on every window ledge.

■ Hundreds of <u>b</u>icyclists <u>b</u>ustled through the downtown streets.

On the lines provided below, write your own examples of pleasing sounds.

_____

_____

_____

_____